THE
30 YEAR
PAYCHECK

THE

30 YEAR
PAYCHECK

*Destruction and Redemption
in Corporate America*

BY SANDER BIEHN

Contents

CHAPTER 1

As long as we are unclear where the road is going, we might as well send up burnt offerings to the gods and then hedge our bets by loosening the pins on our competitor's chariots.

CHAPTER 2

To paraphrase Jesus of Nazareth, "Just as God watches out for the small birds, God also protects the Classics Majors from Duke."

CHAPTER 3

"With proper care, these shoes will last you a lifetime."

CHAPTER 4

"Hog butcher to the world, tool maker, stacker of wheat."

CHAPTER 5

Basically, the idea is quite simple. Prey on your customers' fears, their fear of change and failure, to get them to do what you wanted. This was utterly foreign to me. My previous four years were about eliciting change from the status quo, and finding new ideas for business to better serve customers and make employees more efficient.

We had traveled frantically for over a year and what our life boasted in glamour, it lacked in stability. The Greek philosopher Heraclitus said you can never step into the same river twice because it is always changing. This river had definitely changed and become more turbulent.

We are under attack, the mist is burning off and General Franco's troops have a perfect view of our hideout high up in the hills overlooking Segovia, Spain. A mortar shell lands nearby and my heart goes cold. I can taste the sod it kicks up. I look for the commander. He is laying propped up under a craggily chestnut tree. He's laughing.

Standing on the quad in the rain as the students shuffle by, I have a strange memory. I remember the person I was when I left this place. Now I can hear him. He is screaming out to me in the rain. Our baby is crying and I can't make out what he is saying.

I would rather face the trolls of the real world market who will vote with their pocketbooks than the internal trolls who want to pass on their inner pain.

I started wondering if the time spent in the bar was at all time well spent for my career. What was I working out?

The plane shook violently as we climbed through the storm. Above the cloud bank was that amazing sight I had seen so many winters in Minnesota. The stars were set like diamonds on the blackest sheet of night imaginable.

The last thing I did before I left St Paul was to throw my parka in a garbage bag bound for recycling. As I did so, I saw the tips of my scuffed cordovan shoes sticking up. My wife had jettisoned them as part of the move. They were supposed to last me a lifetime according to the salesman. I could not wear them any longer because the leather was destroyed from misuse, but I refused to get rid of them. I thought about pulling them out of the bag. Something stopped me. In my shirt sleeves I quickly got into my blue Subaru by myself and left. I was bound for Atlanta.

Our move to Atlanta had wiped out our savings in the bank, but the reserves in my heart had grown tenfold.

I dedicate this book to my dad.

Introduction

I Hate Dilbert. For well over a decade, Dilbert has been a lasting figure in corporate America. In his daily cartoon, Scott Adams serves up humor from the cube-farm with his non-descript, crooked-tie protagonist engineer and his snoopy-esque entrepreneurial dog Dogbert. Dilbert skewers the corporate life in every intelligent respect; for example, the penchant to set a meeting first and ask why later. He reminds us of the stupidity of upper management. In his cartoons, management does a self-preserving rain dance instead of looking out the window or asking a front line manager what needs to be done. Avarice and egotism dominate the executives in the comic strip. Meanwhile, we chuckle and bury our heads in our hands laughing because we don't want to cry.

I haven't always disliked Dilbert. I had yellowed clippings of the engineer and his not-so-loveable pooch pinned to my cube fabric like anyone else, but at some point it stopped being funny to me. I know that folks in prison need to keep their chins up so they can endure their sentences. Humor is a great way to do that, but this is different. The analogy is more like a wrongfully imprisoned political activist, working to right societal wrongs, chuckling and laughing over the daily beatings and reprogramming he suffers at the hands of his prison guards. The fact is, Dilbert isn't funny to me.

THE 30 YEAR PAYCHECK

I once heard an executive give a talk where he referenced a Dilbert cartoon and said, "Did you know that Scott is one of ours?" He uneasily beamed with pride. "I didn't know him", he then rationalized. It turns out Adams worked for this man's organization once upon a time. I think Dilbert should make us all feel uneasy. I recently read a post Adams made in The Wall Street Journal. He painted himself as a serial entrepreneur who had failed much more than he succeeded. Dilbert was his crowning achievement. He proudly boasted that he owed his success to two things: Lack of goals and lack of passion. Certainly this was written for shock value. What went through my mind as I read the article was, "Would I give this advice to my children?" That was easy to answer. No!

Some will believe it is just humor, and that humor and satire have always been used to right wrongs in society. I understand that, but there is a personal human toll to what is happening in office buildings around the country. You would never see someone cynically joke about cancer or child abuse. It just isn't tasteful.

Dilbert is part of the problem. Dilbert allows us to continue to believe that there is some immensely stupid, but powerful force that makes us act the way we do. However, instead of declining an invitation to a pointless meeting with a well-reasoned alternative to the sender, we click on the 'accept' button. Tomorrow's Dilbert strip will surely allow us to laugh at and feel superior to this pointless meeting, but we remain paralyzed to start changing the culture.

Ask yourself, what will happen to Dilbert cartoons when things change in the workplace and true collaboration and innovation become the norm? Ask yourself whether the best companies in America resemble Dilbert's world today? Most importantly, ask yourself whether you want to participate in Dilbert's world or work to change it? I believe there is not an option of doing both. Yeah, I still read Dilbert, but I use that few seconds to promise myself that I will work to change the world around me. I will not laugh at the comic, but rather empathize with the spirits of all the real people out there being crushed by the scenarios played out in the panels on the inky pages of The Atlanta Journal Constitution. Here in Atlanta, Dilbert is the only comic that appears in the business section. Why? Is it because anyone not in corporate America won't be able to find any humor in Scott Adam's world? If it was so funny, why wouldn't they?

I am not sure about you, but I cannot live without goals and passion. Everyone has the right to live any way they choose. I choose not to live in Scott Adams' world. But that was not always the case. In fact, I lived there for more than twenty years. And this is my story. It is my story of a career never intended. It is my story of success followed by sharp elbows in the gut. It is my story of being ground down to a pile of dust and then rising like a Phoenix with a crooked tie from the ashes.

Chapter 1

Left Behind

Steam billows from the central HVAC plant adjacent to the Hennepin County Medical Center in Minneapolis, Minnesota. Also known as the HCMC, this is the downtown hospital that cares for the worst of traffic accidents, shootings and home repairs gone haywire. The 94D extended bus slams into one last bone shattering pot hole as it makes its way to the 5th Avenue exit. Even though I have been riding for twenty minutes, I still cannot feel my feet from the cold, and I lightly tap them on the vehicle's slushy floor. From my window seat, I now see the TotalCom tower coming into view. Its warm weather green hue looks more pale in the early morning light of deep winter. People often describe the building as looking like a stalk of fresh asparagus, but in the subzero air it now looks like its frozen cousin from the Jolly Green Giant freezer bag.

Another sales year has begun. Our latest layoff and reorganization behind us, it is time once again to be hopeful. And like the two-faced Roman god Janus, for whom the month of January is named, it is time for us to look forward with enough wisdom to also remember our past. Even though it is now February, we still don't have our quotas. Our sales kick-off was three weeks ago in Las Vegas, but it still feels like the year has not yet begun. I have every reason to be positive. I survived the fall layoff, didn't I?

Walking through the skyway to the asparagus building, I start to feel a bit nervous. This is my second full year as a sales manager and another reorganization has left me managing three people who were once my peers. To make matters worse, my previous boss and mentor was dismissed in the fall and now I was taking his old role-- and may perhaps even be moved into his old office. While I am not usually superstitious, the prospect of moving into the office of a terminated employee, where I had done so many reviews as an account representative, would be just plain spooky. In the elevator, I bump into one of the guys on my team. We exchange pleasantries about the kids and ice hockey. Can he tell I am not feeling like myself?

Thankfully, I can now feel all my toes. My boss and friend, Frank, waltzes into my office. With a hook of his right foot, he nonchalantly closes the door behind him.

This can't be good.

"I wanted to let you know before I tell the rest of the team that I am taking another job." He spits out faster than lightning.

What? He can't do that! He hired me. He is not allowed to leave me behind. How will I negotiate quota relief with another new boss? How will this new sales year have any chance of success for me and my team? Summary executions of management staff hired by the previous sales center VP are all too common. He knows that. He stammers ahead, but I can tell he does not want to spend a lot of time chatting. He has things to do.

Left Behind

After he leaves I look out my seventh floor window. In the distance, an old warehouse building is being demolished to make way for a new condo or office tower. It is 2010 and someone is still pumping money into housing in Minneapolis. God bless him. I suddenly realize, the end is near.

Sounds dire, doesn't it? But it isn't like you think. I don't believe the world is ending, or even my job. But something is fundamentally changing. I suddenly feel very nervous. I feel like I need to get working on an exit strategy.

There are few things like uncertainty that give us a more severe sinking feeling in the gut. But it is also amazing how much we are able to ignore in order to avoid that feeling. In my story, the time to have started worrying was the previous fall when layoffs were being announced. Aside from being a time when leaves dry up, change color and wither, fall is layoff season--at TotalCom anyway.

What is it we were doing (or not doing) that got us to the point of missing our numbers? We all knew the business would need to react with job reductions. We had seen this countless times. Yes, reducing jobs is a desperate measure. With less workforce, it is harder to meet goals that are already being missed, and that is what precipitates layoffs in the first place. It is a vicious cycle that usually leads to another year of downsizing. Sales teams are often shocked by the additional quota they receive the year after a layoff. If you think about it, though, it all makes perfect sense. More must be required of everyone who survives. But that never makes it easy to understand, because it just doesn't seem rational. Resentment is what follows. In the field, we often see this as an organizational problem--as an issue with leadership at headquarters. Rarely do we ever assign any of that ownership to ourselves. What was it about my team's performance last year that contributed to the layoff? What could we have done differently organizationally, or tactically? Did we begin too late? Did we lose deals due to lack of positioning with customer's executives? Did we lose out because our competitors better partnered with ancillary providers? We generally never find out, because nobody ever asks.

At TotalCom, we know these reductions will come in the late fall. Always the same time. This is when someone at headquarters realizes we will not make our business plan. Tap dancing in the big office won't work. It is time to admit defeat and set to work with a plan. The months leading up to the layoff are stressful. Everyone retreats into survival mode. Once the reduction takes place, those who remain are grateful for their jobs and ready to overspend on holiday gifts for the family. One knee jerk decision begets another, and we live as if there is no tomorrow. No one takes a good hard look in the mirror. Instead, our sense of control dwindles and we wonder what will happen next? Paranoia becomes rampant.

But, if we remain in this mode, we never improve our sense of control. If anything, we throw away what little control we have. We rely even more on our superiors to protect us and we do what we can to crush internal competition. As long as we are unclear where the road is going, we might as well send up burnt offerings to the gods and then hedge our bets by loosening the pins on our competitor's chariots. Because so many of us behave in this manner, we merely improve the chances that next year will mean another layoff and more of the same behavior.

There is another way, though. It starts with owning the things we did poorly the year before. It means experimenting with different ideas for our future. Instead of girding ourselves for another bad year, capped with another downsizing and reorganization, we should be imagining how we might do it differently this time.

The beginning of the year is the perfect time to reflect on what did and what did not work the year before, and to enlist help in changing the organization now. Do it in January, and not when it is too late.

If we could only break out of this mode and take a good hard look at our contribution to our fate.

This story is not meant to be cautionary, as much as it is meant to be instructional and redemptive. This tale is about working for a big technology firm for twenty years and what it taught me about fear, imagination and people. Like most workers who have long term tenure in a large company, I surely learned a lot about the industry along the way. But I also learned how to survive almost any situation in order to feed my family. At least, this is how I saw it. Over time I became frozen in place. Acting in a certain way because it was all I knew anymore. I became so jaded that I had forgotten about myself and my talents. I forgot that all I needed to be was me. I didn't need to be anyone else or use my time defeating co-workers in a battle up the corporate pyramid. I was actually sufficient all along. The more I took my eye off of the mirror, the more I acted like the others, the more I languished in jealousy and insecurity, the more I forgot who I was and what abilities I had.   So frequently people bemoan the lack of creativity in corporate America. However, it is not the lack of intelligent and creative people that make it so. It is the stifling environment that emasculates the human asset. *The 30 Year Paycheck* is my story of losing my way and then, eventually, finding it again.

I need to say that, it is not my intention to bash anyone. If anyone deserves a bashing, it is I. Twenty years of my life was spent trying to figure out how to see myself clearly in the mirror, and begin to be myself, not someone I supposed I should be, or someone who just knew how to work the system. I am not advocating that people should or shouldn't work in corporate America. That decision is purely personal and one that each of us must make. I also do not pass judgment on how, or why, organizations are devised and aligned the way they are. There are plenty of books written on that topic. The fact is, be it right or wrong, the organization of large companies takes a human toll on those working there and their loved ones. An entrepreneur recently told me that his wife had nervous break-down after they moved to Atlanta. I immediately assumed it was due to his crazy world in start-up business mode. "No," he said, "Twenty years working for the largest financial institution in the United States did it." Silly me.

I must say that some characters in my story will look pretty mean and others just plain ridiculous, but I am not trying to demonize anyone including my fictional colleagues. Dear reader please bear in mind that these characters have nice parents and families and dogs and cats they love and who love them at home. But this is my story. So, someone has to play the villain. As Shakespeare told us, "…we each have our parts to play." The situations in this book are fictitious, but directionally correct as to how things work in many large companies today. It is presented to give anyone inside or outside of corporate America a flavor of how these organizations work and can be improved.

One thing that I do want to indict is the generally sad state of business writing these days. I read a recent column by a syndicated Chicago columnist cynically describing how to write a business book in a week. Ironically, I had spoken the week before with a colleague who told me about a software package that enables anyone to write a book in just one weekend.

It isn't a matter of how long a book took to write or what formula was followed. It is only important how good the work is. Too many business books fall into a category devised and coined by my teenage daughter, "The Pamphle-book". A "Phamphle-book" is really a pamphlet that gorged itself on junk words and bloated to a two hundred page manuscript. These books are gold for Amazon and Google reviewers and summary writers, as they can easily be condensed to make the casual reader seem like the avid one. Even Malcolm Gladwell's most recent book, *David and Goliath* was reviewed as being two-thirds good-- the last third reading more like a research paper than the normal Gladwellian sharpwitted-ness.

Sorry, this is not a pamphlet-book. My purpose is to consider how to truly thrive in corporate America and what you need to ask yourself each morning to avoid being trapped. But alas, I have no system for doing this though. This book reads more like *Crime and Punishment* or *Moby Dick* (minus the whale anthology near the end). It is my story from start to finish. How I rocketed from 20 to 45 years of age in the world of work and how it changed me. I have no snappy acronyms or "six do's and don'ts" to follow. I start at the beginning and end on my last day working at a corporate behemoth with a new set of ideas and goals for my life.

I would like to believe that I have written this book to inspire others, but I am not sure I totally buy that statement myself. I think I have written this book as a parting love note to a time in my life. It is about something I learned. It is about something it took me a very long time to learn. It is about something I hope will resonate with others and help them on their journey.

Chapter 2

The Unexpected Career

The month of May for a college student is generally a good time of year, especially at Duke University. The leaves are back on the trees, the weather is warm and students are itching to get out of class after another year of studying.

Back in 1990, we seniors were getting our job offers, and it seemed like each day another happy yell was coming from someone or another who had been admitted to Yale Law or Duke Medical School. A much smaller group of us were looking for 'real jobs'. I had proclaimed rather publicly, while standing on top of a picnic bench outside the 'Hideaway', our on-campus bar that I was 'never, ever, ever, ever going to school again.' And I meant it. College had been a breath of fresh air for me allowing me to follow my passions. I majored in Philosophy and Classical Studies. I could not get enough of the ancient world of the Greeks and Romans. But, academia had become a bureaucracy which hindered my spirit. My inability to master the ancient Greek language despite years of study prompted more than one professor to discourage me from majoring in Classics. I wasn't going to have it though, and I marched on, worrying about my all-important double major diploma. While I lived a carefree life, the cost of my privileged education to my parents always stuck in the back of my head. After four years, I was convinced I had learned how to learn, and I looked forward to the freedom of not having a professor or advisor push me around.

THE 30 YEAR PAYCHECK

By May, I was determined to find a job. Something that would pay my keep so that I would no longer burden my parents. I wanted to prove my worth to the greater world by living in a sordid apartment with health insurance and the means to pay for it each month.

I remember quite vividly sitting on the floor in my senior year dorm room staring dumbfoundly at the contents of a large United States Post Office package I had just torn open. "Dear Sir/Madam" a short note read, "your package/letter was sadly involved in a postal accident. This means it was undeliverable. The remains of your package/letter are enclosed..." It went on to explain the insanely small statistical chance that a letter could meet this fate. Sitting before me were the mangled remains of a stack of my resumes and a universal application form for teaching positions at thirty elite boarding schools. I had mailed them a couple of weeks ago and now the deadline had passed. I was going to graduate in less than two weeks with a degree in Classical Studies and Philosophy and my last ditch attempt to get a teaching job at some country club for rich kids in western Massachusetts had just been nullified by a mail sorting machine in Richmond, Virginia. The classicist in me wondered if I was being pursued by the furies for some hubris I surely committed during my years at Duke's gothic containment area for the privileged. Depressed and disheartened, I wondered, "What next?" I couldn't go home. Living in the basement of my parent's place was an option I felt I could not exercise. They had taken out a second mortgage to put my brothers and me through college. The least I could do is not come back and sleep under my tacked up diploma (alas, no money for a proper framing).

The Unexpected Career

Several days later, I bumped into my friend Sabrina. She was a year or two behind me at Duke and was excited about her summer and, as usual, full of spark and bubble. She sensed something was bothering me. I told her about the postal accident, trying to make light of it and my current dismal prospects. She didn't laugh. "What kind of summer jobs have you had?" she asked in a business-like manner. No one had ever spoken to me like this, least of all another student, least of all an underclasswoman. In a stream of consciousness format, I told her what I had done the past few summers. Meanwhile, backpack toting pre-meds paraded before my eyes on their way to Perkins library to cram for their exams.

Among other things, I shared with Sabrina that I had worked most recently as an intern at TotalCom and as a door to door garbage service salesman. This takes some explaining.

My uncle worked at TotalCom as a Sales VP in an office just outside Philadelphia. Though I suspect my dad put him up to it, he offered me a summer internship. July and August were a blur. I commuted forty-five minutes each way from my parent's home to the office in the most hideous traffic imaginable, all for a $5,000 stipend. The job was tediously dull and mostly consisted of searching for faxes that seemed to pour in by the thousands in a noisy copy room. I was under everyone's eye. I usually slept in my car over the lunch hour, and after ten weeks I still had not the faintest idea what was going on there or what people actually did all day. How could all this talk, all these meetings and, most incredibly, all these faxes have anything to do with keeping the world turning and, in return, employees' families fed? I can still hear my uncle's voice as he explained the dress code: "We wear coats and ties, but usually shed the jackets when we get into the office, roll up our sleeves and get to work."

My biggest moment in the sun was at the company picnic that took place in some private campground in Pennsylvania's Pocono Mountains. Several branches of TotalCom converged there for the annual event. As in the days of the ancient Greeks, we feasted and, of course, had games. I was a 'ringer' in a one-on-one basketball tournament. I was faster, quicker, better and, most importantly, younger than the other contestants. However, I was not ready for the real world. These guys were ponderous and lacked skill, but they had sharp elbows and possessed more of one of mother earth's most precious resources: gravity. They also chided me and psychologically ripped me. They feigned injury and then stepped on my foot. That day at the picnic was really my first interaction with a corporate job for a large firm. I felt like I was being lowered rather quickly into a tank full of hungry crocodiles. I saw that the working world might be tedious and dull one minute and then bone-breakingly painful the next, but I shrugged it off. What did I care? In a few weeks, I would return to another year of academic solace and keg parties.

The summer before, I worked with two high school friends, blanketing large neighborhoods in Bucks County, Pennsylvania with flyers, trying to get people to switch their garbage service providers. My buddy's brother, Joe, worked at a large corporate trash hauler in Philly that had decided to make inroads into my more suburban county. They needed critical mass quickly. The big hauler was less expensive. But most of the existing haulers in the suburbs were small mom-and-pop shops. They served the same customers for years. Our family was on a first name basis with our trash haulers, along with our letter-carrier and milkman. Yes, we had a milkman.

My friends and I quickly learned that conversations with potential customers were time consuming and emotional. Everyone wanted to save money, but no one wanted to tell their existing hauler they were leaving. So, our approach was to cover a lot of ground and distribute as many flyers as we could to potential clients without having personal contact. Inside of many suburban homes late at night our flyers were read. By stealth, homeowners cut the throats of their existing suppliers. Letters were discreetly put in the mail. Money was saved and we had an abundance of new customers. We were to receive minimum wage plus $5 per subscription sold. I am sure we wouldn't have gotten the minimum wage if Joe could have found a way around it. We had to keep track of who went where, but when all else failed my friends and I just divided up the money. And there was a lot of it!

I learned that working with friends was fun, but infuriating. We took turns driving and it was always hard to get going on hot summer days. Someone was always complaining-- about the heat, the streets we had chosen or the need to go to the bathroom. The small idiosyncrasies of each of us preyed upon the others. Whatever fun we expected to have with each other, quickly devolved into just another job. We had a lot of freedom and made good money, but sometimes the freedom got the better of us and interfered with the work and thereby the money we could have made.

THE 30 YEAR PAYCHECK

Sabrina took it all in. "Would you like to be a salesman?" she asked. I looked at her with a blank stare. "You have done two sales-type jobs; it just seems like you like that work." I was confused. No one in their right mind wanted to be a salesperson, right? That was the job of last resort, the job with no experience required because no one wanted it. I had no idea at the time that one in ten workers in the US worked in sales. That statistic was the kind of thing you didn't want to think about, like the statistics on road fatalities.

Besides, even had I known that one in ten of us would end up sales-people, it would have just confirmed to me the evil of Capitalism. No one would have pegged me for a Capitalist. I wore ripped clothes, long hair and had scrawled the following lyrics from a Hüsker Dü song on my dorm wall: "All the money you can steal, can't buy a piece of what I feel" I thought I was the ultimate free spirit.

Sabrina was unfazed by the look on my face. She matter-of-factly informed me that two friends of her sister had started a business called Communicate Direct selling telephone systems in Chicago and were looking for sales people.

On any other day of my somewhat notorious college career, I would have politely said, 'no thanks.' But as I sat there in the hot May sun in front of my dorm, thoughts charged through my head. 'Maybe she's right. I have had two jobs and both were sales related. And, one of them was with a technology firm.'

But, 'No!' my inner voice was now screaming. 'This isn't how it goes. You have a Duke diploma. The labor market should be falling all over you. Besides, how in the world is this related to philosophy or the ancient classical world?'

"Ok" I said, with as much enthusiasm as I could muster. "Go to it, Sabrina."

Probably nothing will come of it anyway. 'I will humor her', I thought. 'Ok, Sabrina. I will allow you to try to help me, though I really don't need it. To paraphrase Jesus of Nazareth, "Just as God watches out for the small birds, God also protects the Classics Majors from Duke."'

Six weeks later I found myself pacing in front of the phone in my grandfather's living room in upstate New York, waiting for a call from Chicago. Amos Maraisons (sounds like 'Crayons' with an M) was going to interview me by phone. Graduation itself had gone well and my parents even offered me a little money to go to Greece and Turkey with classmates to see the ancient structures we had studied. With some hesitation, I took the gift that included a flight on discount airliner "Fantasy Airways" and spent six glorious weeks sleeping on beaches, ferry decks and in olive groves while visiting ancient sites. Standing on the mountain top overlooking the ruined town of Delos where the Athenians plundered the treasury and took the money to Athens in the 500's BCE, I wondered what New York be like if all the money were to go elsewhere in a day. I suppose the people would follow, just like they did on Delos. This is how ghost towns are born. Wind and sand blew in my face. The boat waited below. I too would leave Delos now and head to Chicago. This is where we moved the money after the Greeks, Romans, Popes, British and American Colonists moved it to New York. The money was now in Chicago, at least the money offered to me. I would banish all other cities and make that my new home.

While I was overseas, I was offered a last minute job in Manhattan-- a $15,000 yearly stipend to work at a Center for Classical Studies. I couldn't afford to live anywhere on that pay, let alone in Manhattan. It would mean I would need to ask my parents for help and that wasn't going to happen.

Back in New York, the telephone rang and my hand began to sweat. I answered the phone and heard Nancy, Amos's assistant, confirm to him that I was on the line.

Amos got right down to business. I answered his questions as best I could, but to this day I cannot remember exactly what he asked. It was the tone I recall. I only know that I would have rather been back on that basketball court with my uncle's top salesman putting his knee into my thigh than spend any more time on the phone with Amos. Amos made him look like a pussycat. The questioning was brutally 'real life' for a romantic scholar like me. Amos concluded by asking me what was the largest purchase I ever made. I froze. Just about every purchase I made to date had been $17 or less.

"You never purchased a bike?"

No.

"Or a fridge for your dorm room"

No.

The questioning went on. Finally I lied that I had bought a stereo. I just wanted to get past it, but it got worse. He started asking me how I felt about the purchase and how the salesperson convinced me to buy it.

The Unexpected Career

My obfuscations of the truth were so convoluted I had trouble breathing, let alone keep track of my fable. He ended by making the point that nothing gets done without a salesperson. I quietly agreed and I perceived the feeling of a sharp elbow going into my gut.

"Never forget, Sander: nothing gets done without a salesperson. Sales is an honorable profession."

Listening to my inner voice, I thought, 'who is fibbing now?'

An offer letter arrived a week later signed by Nancy's swirling female script in the name: Amos Maraisons. I was offered a base salary so low that I later learned I could have been collecting food stamps. No matter, it was more than the New York job and I was sure I could live more cheaply in the Windy City. I would receive that salary for six months in a probationary period while I learned the business by job shadowing the entire staff of seven people. But the kicker was that after six months, I could make a commission of 10% on everything I sold. The letter went on to say that my earning potential was expected to be $40,000 the first year. This figure was considerably higher than even the best jobs my undergraduate classmates had been offered. The only trouble was, mine was not guaranteed, and to this day I do not know where Amos conjured up that figure.

Later, I realized that this job was the greatest purchase I had ever made. I bought into being a salesman. I was sold. I sold my education, dreams and carefree existence for the potential of $40,000 per year. I quickly accepted the job. What's the worst that could happen? If I failed, I could come home. Plan C was to move in with my brother who lived in Boca Raton, Florida.

I never thought through the other option, though...what if I succeeded? Would I spend the rest of my life in Chicago? If not, how long would I stay? What was it that I ultimately wanted to do? If I didn't know the answer to that question, what was my plan to find out?

That's the way it is when you are young. The real question I should have been asking myself is, 'How could I ever find my place in the world if I succeeded?'

I stuffed the acceptance letter into the map holder on the door of my 1983 red Ford Tempo, where it remained for many years. It was transferred to my next car and the car after. I suppose I wanted it to remind me of the momentous decision I made, the bullet of unemployment that I had dodged. Pointedly, I lost the letter my last year in Minnesota right when things hit bottom. But let's not go there just yet. Instead, let's take a closer look at my transition from school to work. Let's watch the plane roll down the runway; destination unknown.

Chapter 3

My Departure in three short acts:

Act I:

Most of my classmates had either been admitted to graduate schools or were employed. I was one of the final hold-outs. But, there was another like me. His name was Steve. He also planned to come to Europe. To make extra pocket money we both headed up to the Adirondack Mountains in upstate New York to help my older brother open a summer camp his employer owned. We lived in my grandfather's cabin and worked all day in the cold and rain. It was the height of black-fly season. Steve had no job and no prospects either. He didn't even have Amos Maraisons calling him from Chicago about a job as a salesman. Most likely, Steve wouldn't have answered the call even if he did.

I cashed the check for my work in New York and drove south to my parent's house with my friend Steve. We were to stay one day in Pennsylvania and then my dad was to drive us to JFK airport for our big European adventure. I felt like a millionaire. I tried to imagine a whole $40,000. What would I do with it all? How many times did $17 (the mean of my purchases to date) divide into $40,000. It was unthinkable. More importantly, I was also 'off the list'. Everyone now had a job or a school to go to that fall...with the one exception of Steve.

In fairness, I probably gloated a bit too much on scoring that job. Steve and I had a rallying cry of 'unemployment' that bonded us, but once I left 'camp unemployed' it must have been pretty dismal pickings around the campfire for him. On the other hand, Steve wasn't doing much to find a job. He spent more time tucked away in the corner on the phone with his mom and dad than he did looking for a job. We quarreled more and more as the Europe trip neared. The night before the trip, we went to bed early but I could not sleep. I was looking through my textbooks at all the monuments I would see. I was looking at the temple where the Pithia spoke riddles to visitors at Delphi when Steve came in the room. I had heard him on the phone in the other room talking to his parents a few minutes before.

"Dude," he said, "I'm not coming. I just had my mom book a ticket back home to New Mexico from JFK tomorrow."

In principle, this was fine. However, I was about to make my first international flight, first to Rome and then on to the Pela Inn in Athens, via transportation as yet not confirmed. I then had to find my friends in Athens. I was 22 and had never been outside the country except a trip to Toronto to see my mom's friend from grad school. It doesn't seem scary now, but it was then. I had no idea what I was getting into.

My father who can be a bit gruff, got mad at Steve. He ripped the poor guy. My dad obviously was worried for me. He cared, and saw this as my departure in several ways. I now am a parent of two kids rapidly approaching their teens. I still care for them and their feelings like I did when they were babies. Watching them leave home most certainly will fill me with the same emotions. I plan on being every bit like my dad.

My Departure in three short acts:

Six weeks and a trip on the orient express from Istanbul to Venice later, I met my dad outside customs at JFK. I felt sad to be home. I knew I needed to head to Chicago in a week and start my job.

Act II:

I went to the shoe store with my dad a few days before I had to leave for Chicago. He was convinced that if I was going to be a salesman I needed a pair of cordovans and he was going to buy them for me. Since my interview with Amos, I started noticing salespeople and how they behaved. The older gentleman who greeted us at the door of the shoe store in my hometown was pleasant and well-dressed in a faded pin-striped suit.

"Cordovans", my dad explained, and he pointed at my feet which were adorned in shredded basketball high-tops.

All the sizes pinched my foot, which were used to wearing high-tops or, more recently, sandals made of recycled tire tread, purchased in the Athenian Plaka. I picked a pair that seemed the right size and the salesman smiled. He looked my dad straight in the eye and said, "With proper care, these shoes will last him a lifetime."

He then stood next to me in front of the mirror and grinned. He looked at my shoes. I looked at him. I wondered what I had gotten myself into. Another liberal arts major had entered the working world. I was a total success now that I had the cordovans in a box and under my arm. I looked back at the salesperson as we left the shop. He was still smiling and waved, but what was he thinking? I looked away and then looked back. He was talking to the woman behind the counter and glancing up from his huge gold watch. For the first time, I really wanted to know what was on a salesman's mind. Was I already being altered?

Act III:

Without too much fanfare I drove away from my home in my red ford Tempo filled to the brim with everything I owned. I drove swiftly to put miles quickly between me and my home town. I figured the sooner I got to Chicago, the sooner this would be over. This is how I deal with change. I try to get through it as fast as I can, sometimes at the expense of learning from the experience.

I figured the sooner I got to Chicago, the sooner I would be transformed and happy. Then I could shelve the frivolity of being a college student and start sharpening my elbows. I never imagined that gravity would slow me down. I drove straight to Ann Arbor, Michigan where an old Duke acquaintance named Mary lived. She was about to start her senior year. It seems so ridiculous in this digital world in which we live, but I had arranged to stay at her parent's house for the night entirely through stamped letters and mailboxes. No email, smart phone or GPS to guide me, it seems like navigation by stars and astrolabe in this day and age.

Mary's parents viewed me with great interest. They were extremely nice to me. They fed me a delicious meal. Afterwards, we discussed my new vocation and destination. It seems everyone in Michigan has lived in Chicago at one time or another. They were shocked to hear that I had never been there. Before bed I snuck outside and took a walk down their suburban lane in my bare feet, careful to

My Departure in three short acts:

keep the door cracked so I could re-enter. I looked down the broad street with new eyes. I had grown up on similar type of street, but somehow I started looking at the houses in Michigan in a new way. Who lived here? What did they do from 9-5 each day? How much did the house cost? Did they have any kids?

I dreamt that night about Grant and Lincoln Park in Chicago. Mary's parents had described them to me with some fondness. In my dreams an impenetrable line of buildings bordered the beautiful park. I was standing on a lush open plain wondering how to enter the city, but not really sure I wanted to. Behind me the roaring gray ocean of Lake Michigan swelled. I was to be shocked by the azure blue of the great lake in the coming months.

The next day I unexpectedly slept in. By the time I got up, Mary's dad was at work. Her mom saw me off with a big breakfast, a packed sandwich and a few peaches. I would never see Mary again. I am sure I wrote a thank-you letter, though. I wonder how many friendships end like that? With a thank-you letter. I can't think of a better way.

I again drove quickly to put distance between Mary's house in the suburbs and my new destination. Coming out of Gary, Indiana, the road became incredibly wide and busy with seemingly countless lanes. Trucks took up most of the road. It was rush hour. I had timed that perfectly. I moved at a crawl for almost two hours. I didn't notice the temperature gauge on the dash climbing. It had to be 95 degrees outside. Suddenly the car sputtered and died.

Ford's symbol for overheating is a temperature gauge. It was lit up red on the dash now. The trucker behind me put on his flashers and jumped out. Wordlessly he assisted me in pushing the car into the center median. I had no idea what to do next. The Sears Tower dominated the hazy horizon. The other buildings seemed to be worshipping her on their knees. Waves of heat wafted off the cars and road on either side of me. I popped open the hood to let the car cool down. I still had no idea what to do. What does one do in a situation like this? It was hot so I took off my shirt and leaned against the front bumper. The hood provided shade, despite the hot engine. The cars and trucks crawled both ways in seemingly endless lines, five lanes wide on either side. I still had no idea what to do. So I decided to not do anything. I sat there shirtless and waited for the sun to set. For those two hours I smiled and savored my last moments of youth and ignorance. I didn't even notice the traffic slowly picking up and thinning out. I eventually closed the hood and tried the ignition. The car started! Resurrected, I entered the city.

Chapter 4

The City of Broad Shoulders

"Hog butcher to the world, tool maker, stacker of wheat." So begins Carl Sandburg's 'Chicago' poem. I pinned a replica of Sandburg's hand written copy of the poem onto the bathroom door in my Chicago studio apartment on Daiken Street. Sandwiched between Boy's Town, a nascent and growing gay community and an immigrant Spanish neighborhood, I felt like a serious target when I walked down the street in any direction.

"I have seen your painted women under the gaslamps," or so says Carl Sandburg.

Around the corner on Sheridan was a Spanish bar, bakery and market. Across the street was a Chinese dry cleaner, a small convenience store that sold liquor and the Sheridan 'L' stop. Another dank bar with a pool table was connected to the station. There was also a currency exchange and small fruit and vegetable stand that sold soap and toilet paper. In the 'L' stop lobby there was a giant red crane game where you could try your luck to win little stuffed animals. Across Irving Park Road at Sheridan there was a hospital and a bit down the street was the city cemetery and a gas station.

This seemed to me to be a perfect place to live. If you counted the greasy Greek diner on Broadway, the opposite direction down Daiken, and the auto garage next to my apartment, there was very little I needed that I could not reach by walking 200 feet. But, from the beginning, there were small signs this was not a very safe place. The enormous rat traps near the dumpster out back, the sign in English and Spanish in the bar window that read "Do not bring weapons into this bar", and the creepy people who roamed the halls and rode the antiquated open air elevator with a folding accordion door in my building. When my parents eventually visited, they sat on my second-hand stained brown couch and had difficulty finding words. My mom kept saying "It's nice" over and over in an extremely unconvincing way.

My choices for an apartment were limited by my salary. Before I started my search I calculated my take home pay after taxes. Pennsylvania Judge Isaac Gott's daughter Margie was living in Chicago trying to make a go of it as a writer, along with her lay-about poet boyfriend. My dad and Zeke were best friends, so I stayed at her apartment near the Damen 'L' stop when I first got to town. She helped me take a practical approach to what I could afford. Margie wisely counseled me to find something near an 'L' stop. It was good advice, but the apartment hunter needed to take me through some rather seedy neighborhoods to find something that fit the bill both literally and figuratively.

Leaving the interstate in the beat up Toyota of my apartment hunter, one of my first memories is seeing a shirtless woman standing in front of a shuttered Amoco gas station pouring water over her head from a plastic bottle.

I might as well add, by way of giving closure, that the apartment building I lived in burned down shortly after I left. I had eventually made some friends in that building. There was a really nice guy from Michigan named Scott who lived across the hall with his girlfriend.

She was looking for modeling work and he worked the night shift as a pastry chef. Each morning Scott won his honey a new stuffed animal at the giant, red crane game in the L lobby, before buying a 40 ounce bottle of beer to wind down with in front of their TV. I often met him coming home as I headed off to work. It was strange to see a guy with a paper bag beer at that hour.

Scott introduced me to another young guy who lived downstairs. I never had a good feeling about him and I cannot even remember his name. He had no furniture in his apartment. What few things he possessed were piled up in the corners. Anyway, he eventually got delinquent with his rent. One evening, he walked to the gas station on the corner of Broadway and Irving Park and bought a bucket of gas (I am pretty sure that is normally frowned upon), walked back to the building, poured it on the floor of his room and lit a match. The person living in my old apartment died.

"The Nikkei average is down along with the London FTSE in early trading…" Public radio Chicago WBEZ says, "Wake up sleepyhead!"

I take a quick shower, eat some cornflakes with sliced plantains on top (I had mistaken them for bananas at the Spanish market), and pull my cordovans from the shoebox. I carefully put them on feeling the momentous weight of, 'they should last him a lifetime', descend upon me. Ok, this is it. Time to go. The hallway is thick with trapped heat and samplings of the questionable lifestyles of each tenant on the hall. The accordion doors on the elevator slam and the lift lowers. On the street, I feel in my pocket for my key as the security door slams behind me against a block of wood that someone has put there to prop it open. The air feels hot already, and any sense of freshness is just a hint. A northbound train squeals around the bend into the Sheridan station above me. Directly under the tracks, an auto mechanic with a filthy shirt smokes a cigarette, entirely immune to the ear-splitting decibels of steel wheels on the track coming from above. I head nervously to the Sheridan station. Dropping a token into the machine, I swing through the mechanical arms and walk up the stairs. The summer heat has bubbled up the creosote in the planks that make up the reputedly burn-proof platform. I look at my fellow travelers. These people look a lot like me. They are dressed for desk jobs. One guy reads the Chicago Tribune, a woman tries to discreetly pull at her stockings around her lower right thigh. I see her. No one much looks at anyone else. The train arrives and we cram into an already very full car. The train lurches forward. From a stainless steel metal box microphone at the back of the car, the conductor calls out the stops in garbled, emotionless, Midwest English. He reminds us that there is, "no smoking, eating, drinking or radio playing allowed." Belmont? Fullerton! Got that one. We go underground and then come up and go through a huge building that creates a canyon around us and blocks out the sun. The train stops. This is normal. There is a lot of traffic this time of day on the tracks. Suddenly, I smell... hotdogs? Yes, hotdogs. The smell is becoming overwhelming and the cornflakes and plantains suddenly begin to rumble uncomfortably in my gut. We finally begin to move. I look back. "Oscar Meyer" is printed in huge letters on the side of the building. The next thing I see are huge, dull, concrete apartment complexes.

The City of Broad Shoulders

Margie told me about this place. It is Cabrini Green. It is one of the largest urban housing projects in the US, and about the most dangerous place to be at any time of day in Chicago. Downtrodden figures walk the sidewalks. Kids run across streets. Women look from balconies. Many of the apartments are boarded up. Signs of fire are everywhere. Cabrini Green becomes the visible symbol for me of my alternative. If I don't succeed as a salesman, I will end up in Cabrini Green. I am sure that will really leave my mom speechless. But worse, the projects become a symbol of failure. People there have obviously failed, my 22 year old brain tells me. Today, the glimmers of life don't seem so bad, though, from the train. Broad smiles and big embraces on the sidewalk.

No matter.

This place becomes my anti-life and I study it each day from the train. The recurring smell of hotdogs and then 'the projects', my nemesis. My sensory reminder that I am only one paycheck away from utter financial collapse and failure.

I exit at my L stop in the river north and start navigating my way to the start of my career. The day is young, but the city is starting to stink already. I see a large rat run behind a dumpster crammed and battered in an alley. I am navigating by north/south east/west coordinates. Chicago is so orderly in that way. It is a perfect grid. On a clear night from an airplane it looks like the fanciful imagination of a graphic artist. Perfect squares extend westward from Lake Michigan hindered only by the Chicago River and a few other dark spots around parks or railroad lines.

I peer intently at the street names, and, more significantly, the numbers that sit on the end of each green sign giving me coordinates. I round a corner with some speed, still peering up, and surprise a group of workers. They are laying new sidewalk cement and I step directly into the wet glop destroying the smooth surface. My one cordovan is covered. I stop and scrape what I can off on the curb and hustle on my way. "If you take proper care of them, these shoes will last a lifetime...", I hear in the back of my head. My brief life passes before my eyes.

Emotionally exhausted, I arrive at the upstairs loft office of Communicate Direct like a new Greek recruit on the plains outside of Troy. Nancy, the assistant, is not there yet but a young, yet rough looking woman named Florin is. She smokes a thin cigarette and argues over the phone with someone named Jane. Amos comes out of the back room carrying a box marked 'Fujitsu' and says, "You must be Sander. Can you give me a hand with this?"

I help him move the box and a few others like it into his Toyota Highlander that is parked in a tow-away zone below. His emergency flashers blink yellow in what is left of the morning light. No one is on the street and it is noiseless, save the L train that straddles the street above Franklin, with its eardrum busting screech. We go back upstairs and he shows me my desk. Florin has programmed a scratched phone on my desk to read "Sanders". I don't point out the error for a week. When I do she apologetically changes it by banging some obscure code on the keypad. The whole process takes less than a minute. The desks are arranged on either side of the office with a long aisle down the center. It is remarkably like a church and is even aligned east west. These details may puzzle or astound an archeologist 2,000 years in the future, but for now it is just the place I work. Five desks line either side of the room and the last ones are piled with boxes. They are obviously vacant. Nancy's desk breaks the symmetry at the front of the room and arches in an L shape to face the entrance that meets the stairwell that comes up from Franklin Street below.

Amos explains that he needs to get to a job-site and will spend more time with me tomorrow morning. In the meantime, he asks me to take inventory of a bunch of brochures that are packed in boxes. He wants me to figure out how many we have and what needs to be ordered. He also wants me to read a few manuals. One has the big red letters AVT on the front and underneath Digital Voice Mail System. The other simple reads: "Panasonic: Digital Business Systems." He also tosses the largest phone directory book of yellow pages I have ever seen in my life on my desk.

"Here is your territory," he smirks. "Oh yeah, and this is for you."

He rummages through his desk and throws me a copy of Zig Ziglar's *Secrets of Closing the Sale.* He grabs his leather briefcase in one hand and another phone sized box in the other. His car keys swing between his upper and lower jaw. "I'll see you tomorrow" he says between his teeth.

Florin has finished with Jane and is now talking to a guy named Harlan. She had extinguished her cigarette surreptitiously when Amos entered and she is now relighting the stub that she had stowed in a drawer. Harlan is talking to Florin from his 'car phone' and explains he will be in front of the building in a minute. Florin promises to meet him downstairs. She finishes the call, and walks over to me. Her head is cocked and she is smiling. She interrogates me, as if I am a new specimen at the zoo. Where do I live? How did I get there? What do I think of Chicago?.... I answer politely, and shyly ask if there is a bathroom. I really want to get the cement off my cordovans, although it appears to have dried to a paste. By the time I get back from the 'washroom,' as Florin calls it, she is gone. I rummage a pen and clean tablet of paper from the desk of Xavier (pronounced 'X-Avier'). He is Amos' business partner. I sit down to start with the brochures. Brochures? Brosures? Brosurres? Is it possible I have a degree from Duke and I am unclear how to spell brochures? I stop short. I don't think any of the reading I have done by ancient writers and philosophers in the past four years has required me to even think of the word 'brochure', let alone spell it.

Just then the door swings open and a large woman with flaming red hair walks in. She has a huge purse and a paper bag marked with a restaurant logo. She smiles and we do introductions. She knows everything about me, and begins to provide some practical information about the office as she pulls a Styrofoam clam shell from her bag and places it in a college dorm-sized refrigerator behind her desk. How had I not noticed that mini-fridge before? We chat for a few minutes, and then it is obvious she wants to get to work. Her desk has the only computer in the entire room. She has fired it up while we were chatting and now she takes a handwritten note from her plastic inbox and begins to type wildly.

I try to read the AVT manual, but I am lost almost at once. The words are not difficult, but I cannot seem to process what they are saying or, more importantly, why are they saying what they do. The description is dry as dirt and I feel as if I am about to fall asleep at my desk.

The City of Broad Shoulders

Somehow, I make it until lunch. Nancy pulls out her clamshell. I walk up the aisle and ask her where to eat. She recommends a number of places in the neighborhood. All sound rather pricey. I smile and head down the stairs. I walk the opposite direction of the places Nancy has recommended in the general direction of Cabrini Green. I cross a large street and see a small diner. Inside, it is packed with men in hard hats ordering at a counter. I squeeze into a swivel chair that moves only ten degrees in either direction. I look up at the selection and, more importantly, the prices. I settle on a plate of fries and bowl of chicken noodle soup. The total is under $2, and with a copious blob of ketchup it feels like a well-rounded meal. This combo becomes my stand-by when I am in the office and haven't remembered to bring a peanut butter and jelly sandwich for lunch.

Afterward, I walk down Marquette Street looking for a bank. There are no banks in my neighborhood, and opening an account near the office sounds like a solid plan. I have a folded cashier's check in my wallet that I had withdrawn from my PSFS account back in Pennsylvania. It is for a whopping $1,937 which seems like a healthy sum to me. I walk into the Marquette bank, and a tired looking clerk opens the account. I feel offended that my $1,937 doesn't seem important to him. After all, I can go anywhere with my $1,937.

No one else returns to the office that afternoon, at least, not before five. Nancy silently works and I read manuals and stack brochures. The clock on the phone mercifully moves to 4:58. I begin counting to 120 slowly. Nancy begins packing up. We walk out together. She heads south to the regional train station toward the suburbs. I walk to my L stop, drop in a token, and make my way back to Daiken Street. My one shoe is starting to crack from the cement accident. It is probably ruined.

When I arrive home I marvel at how tired I am. I consider how little I really did that day and wonder how it could sap so much energy. I prepare hotdogs for dinner and wash them down with a 16 oz Old Style beer. As it says in Genesis: So ended the first day.

Those first months were a whirlwind for me. I really need to hand it to Amos Maraisons. He ran a small shop, but he took care to think about my on-boarding, and, from the beginning, he was trying to figure out how to differentiate his business from his competition. He and Xavier had worked in New York for a large manufacturer of phone equipment as a sales and sales-engineer duo. When they broke away and started to sell in Chicago, they immediately signed up to partner with Illinois Bell. This gave them some instant credibility in The Windy City. They also hired a hybrid telemarketer-cum-starving-artist type. It was a great fit. Dexter Baxter was a life-long thespian and was trying to break into directing in Chicago's vibrant theater scene. He came in the office only when he needed the cash or wasn't busy and helped me 'dial the phone book'. His convincing theatrical voice obfuscated the fact that he had about as much idea as to what all this technical gear actually did as did I. His goal was always "get the appointment."

My on-boarding was a thorough immersion in the business that Amos devised in waves. The first wave was with the technicians and the in-staller, Florin. I moved boxes and learned to pull wire both in suburban office buildings and ratty Chicago warehouses. The techs taught me the wire color codes of a 66-block and how to use a 'punch-down tool' to secure connections. I hung phone switches on plywood backboards in phone rooms and learned through tedious repetition how to program phone systems. Lunch now consisted of greasy Italian beef sandwiches in every dirty corner of the city. Sometimes I also went out for drinks with the guys. I remember the first time. We had just been paid and we went to some dive. Everyone was drinking beer with bourbon chasers. After two rounds, I excused myself. I can't recall the train ride home, I just remember waking up on Saturday morning cursing myself for missing half the precious weekend by whooping it up on Friday night. The work was exhausting and I constantly felt like it was robbing me of my life's energy. I refused to believe that this was my life.

Florin was my constant companion during that first wave. I got a lift with her to most places. Early each morning we met at the Amoco around the corner from the Communicate office. Florin had a special friend who worked there, and they flirted constantly. She had a crush on him. The only problem was that he was married. I felt sorry for Florin. Each day, we loaded the boxes from the office. Then Florin bought a package of thin cigarettes at the Amoco and we were off to the first installation site. Part of the job was training clients on how to use their new phones and voice mail systems. My first training session was a disaster. A room full of eyes were on me, everyone was quiet waiting for my instruction. I knew how to use the system backwards and forwards, but I could not spit out a coherent sentence. Learning to speak to a group was a skill that I would need to develop. The next month or so cured that. I logged hundreds of training sessions, from individual tutorials with executives to large groups of factory workers who probably could not understand English. After about four months of this, I was cleared to start selling. My paycheck just barely covered my expenses, but it didn't matter. I was so exhausted that, on the weekends, I could think of nothing better than sitting in my apartment reading Russian novels, or heading to the playground for a pick-up game or two of basketball. Sunday nights were always rough. Laying on my futon on the floor of my apartment, I would listen to the ambulances, shuttling the city's broken and bruised to the emergency room of the hospital around the corner on Irving Park Road. I wondered how many other bruised and broken people like me lay awake in the dark with no screaming sirens and red lights to shuttle us to care.

Amos and Xavier opened a retail store on North Avenue. Ingenious. The store was crammed between an upscale home store and a beauty salon. Sitting on the edge of the gentrified part of Lincoln Park, the rent was dirt cheap yet the store was on the radar of the wealthier young people who lived in the next neighborhood. We abandoned the office in the river north and crammed into the windowless area behind the retail front where even increasing the wattage of our light bulbs did little to make it seem like anything other than a cave. Desks were replaced with a long bench and when we were all in the office we sat packed in like sardines. Talking loudly on the phone was the only way to keep your train of thought. As a salaried employee, I was asked to work weekends at the store to start learning how to sell. I was instructed to ask anyone I spoke to about their place of work and if we could assist with their phone gear. Any leads I got, I was allowed to do the follow up. Thus began my transition from Florin's team to my role as a salesperson.

We stocked the retail floor with just enough interesting inventory to pull technoids in off the street. We also attracted our fair share of nefarious figures too, who sometimes either shoplifted or, periodically, robbed us in earnest. We were also selling a new service that Illinois Bell had rolled out: mobile phones. They were expensive, huge, and ugly. I think minutes cost between $.20 and $.30 each. Many months later, I went on a sales call with Xavier to Milwaukee. The snow was falling heavily and we were about the only car on the road. His 4-wheel drive Toyota made Xavier almost fearless. He spoke nearly the entire ride on his 'car phone'. As I calculated the cost of this conversation, it staggered me. But this was the way Amos and Xavier kept the business propelling forward. They each worked non-stop and multi-tasked all day.

One fall Saturday a man dressed in Docksiders, khakis and an Izod shirt came into the store. I showed him our selection of really cool cordless phones, but he wanted something bigger. He wanted the ability to have multiple lines and put people on music hold in his 4,000 square foot brownstone mansion. He explained that he worked at the Board of Trade and had had a particularly good quarter trading there. He had just purchased the house and he wanted it to have all the latest equipment. I explained to him how our Panasonic Digital Business System worked and he wanted one. I worked up the price including a generous amount of labor to wire his house. I was sure he would never want to buy it. But for him $2,700 was not a big sum (at least that day it wasn't). He agreed to the price and put down a 50% down payment. This was my first phone system sale. Amos and Xavier could not have been more pleased and I was taken completely off of the installation team rotation and started spending my days cold calling.

I had finished the Zig Ziglar's sales book. I found the entire thing reprehensible and vile. Zig seemed to treat the human buyer as a slab of meat that could be seasoned, flattened and cooked to perfection by the discerning salesperson who wanted his money. Having read Plato and Kant, I knew people were more complicated than this, but there was the best seller, Zig Ziglar, teaching me circus tricks like the 'Columbo Close' ("Just one more question, ma'm.") Several years later when our sales team had burgeoned to ten, we all went to see Zig live at the Masonic Temple off Michigan Avenue. It was crazy. People worshipped this man, but I could feel the sleaze from 1,000 feet away in the back row.

As a protest, I decided to read the entire book in a beatnik cafe on Belmont. I don't remember the name of the place, but it was the king of cool. People sat and smoked and drank coffee all day, writing poetry or re-reading James Joyce's *Ulysses*. I sauntered in with Zig and sat as conspicuously as possible so everyone could see what I was reading. No one said anything, but I drove at least several starving poets out of the cafe and back onto the mean streets.

I was a bonafide sales person now, but definitely the lowest person on the totem pole. Amos and Xavier sold full time. Both took me on calls to see their biggest clients to show me how it was done. Amos proudly introduced me as a Duke grad, and the first member of his college hire program. I only wonder what the customers thought of that.

The other salesperson was Jane. Jane rarely came in the office. Amos and Xavier hired her the spring before I arrived. She was young, with short red hair and freckles. She was from Michigan and had been hired by TotalCom to work in Chicago when she graduated from Michigan State. I am not sure how she met Amos and Xavier, but her polish and big-company poise were intimidating to me. Jane was extremely good to me when I first arrived. She took me to dinner and the movies. Although when I started getting leads from Dexter instead of them going to her, she was less than pleased. Jane showed me how to fill out an expense form. Amos taught me to never work on that during the workday or he would reject it. Jane taught me the art of a 'three call close'. Amos was constantly trying to perfect the 'one call close' or better yet to sell over the phone. Amos and Jane represented the two polar opposites in selling as far as I knew at the time. Amos was much more about giving the clients what they wanted and moving on. Jane wanted to make sure she built a long lasting relationship by remembering her customers' birthdays and by bringing them chocolate and flowers.

I dove in at the phone banks armed with the humongous Yellow Pages Directory and a pad of paper. "Can I please speak with the person who is in charge of your phone system?" This was my one question. Who knew so many different responses could come from a receptionist who answered my call, when I asked only that one question? Statistically, the most common response was, "we don't need your help" followed by the click of the receiver. Dexter taught me to withstand the rejection. He suffered it constantly. All the while, he threw a squeeze ball against the wall and doodled suggestive pictures of unknown beauties on his pad of paper. Whenever he had a theater production, he would disappear for months. Amos allowed me to use his follow up sheet and paid Dexter a bounty if I could get a successful appointment.

My approach was somewhere between Jane and Amos's. I wasn't as direct as Amos on the phone despite Amos's coaching to get to the point.

"No one wants you to waste their time," he told me.

I sometimes spent too much time talking to lonely hearts who had a lot of needs, but no money. I possessed discipline, however. I set call goals that Amos assured me would yield appointments and, thereafter, lead to sales. This is the simple idea of a 'sales funnel'. At Communi- cate, it was never theoretical. It came true on a daily basis. The ritual of calling people over and over and over until the threshold number of contacts were made, always yielded results. It also made me feel so dirty by the end of the day that I needed a second shower. By the spring thaw, I was making commission money and was learning the city like the back of my hand. I knew every shortcut and how to beat traffic at any hour of the day. When the city started tearing up the Kennedy expressway the following summer, I began learning the backstreets. I don't think there is inch of asphalt in the city of Chicago that I have not driven on at one point or another. Amos and Xavier were pleased with my progress. I was the bet that paid off. Increasingly, Jane was the bet that didn't. She left in the spring and I took over her accounts. They tended to be larger and her clients continued to buy from us.

The City of Broad Shoulders

One of the accounts was Michaels' Cooperage. This company made barrels that were used for shipping rendered meats from packing and processing plants. The company owner, Bob Michaels, was a second generation businessman and third generation Irish American, and had squandered his money almost to the point of putting the company out of business. At the last minute, an Asian company stepped in and bought him out. The man who ran the company now was Arthur Kwong. Bob and Arthur were good friends and now the business was expanding. These two middle age men loved to travel to Asia together and really missed Jane. They insisted we talk business at a Chinese restaurant in Chinatown on a regular basis. The conversations always turned to my romantic life. I was happy to tell them about my girlfriend who was shortly to become my wife. After all, I always got a new order at the end of the lunch. After one such lunch they suggested I bring my girlfriend to the next get together. That is one lunch I won't forget. How could I have been so naïve? When you are young you don't know how much your youth is worshipped. I had no idea they just wanted a lunch with a pretty young girl. But, by bringing Laurie with me, I fulfilled the need they missed after Jane's departure. It wasn't until years later that I fully understood.

My bank account was steadily growing and so was Communicate. I got married and moved into a larger apartment a few blocks from Daiken Street. These days that neighborhood is prime real estate, but back then it was still rather marginal. The El Gato Negro bar around the corner regularly had a broken plate glass window on Sunday mornings and the drug dealers were being busted on Saturday nights in the parking lot in front of my Laundromat on Irving Park and Southport. Laurie was enrolled in Law School at Northwestern and I was footing the bill with my burgeoning sales successes.

Communicate now had six salespeople. Mike came from the copier sales business and had a rolodex list of clients he could now call on for telephone systems. He belonged to a health club across the street from the Sears Tower and we went down there together after work to play basketball and have a few beers. Aiden McAllen had just moved back from Los Angeles where he had tried to make it in show business. Instead he toiled as a bag thrower at LAX airport and eventually came home with his girlfriend and got married. Aiden insisted we play golf to keep our salesman shtick going. Mike, Aiden and I would sneak out early on Friday, much to Amos's chagrin, to play some golf north of the city. Going to the suburbs always healed my heart. I felt like I was connecting with a previous life. A life that was carefree and easier than the one I had now. The trips always ended with long lines of traffic heading back to the city. Mike and Aiden were my friends and constant companions.

By this time, I had worn about a quarter-sized hole in one of my cordovans and one day the sole detached entirely from the shoe. I had to go to an appointment in a couple of hours. Always resourceful, my two friends used markers and masking tape to reconnect my shoe so it looked almost normal. I got a new sole put in after that. After all, these shoes were going to last me forever.

Other new salespeople at Communicate introduced me to a different side of the profession. If Zig Ziglar was slippery, then Pete Bronson was quicksilver mixed with oil. Pete was a middle aged guy, who Amos and Xavier hired away from Communicate's chief competitor. Pete sat next to me on the long bench. He wore cheap suits and smelled of too much cologne. I began noticing that his eyes would wander to my lead sheet. Several times after that, I got to a customer location only to hear that they had already met with Pete. Pete didn't have a whole lot of pride. He was going to get a sale by hook or by crook. I remember several times when he approached me privately to ask for a loan until payday. Usually, he was good for the money after the second request for a payback. I felt sorry for him. My last year at the firm I made an enormous sale. The commission check was greater than $30,000. When we were paid that Friday, he leaned over to me.

"So, are you getting that big check today?" he asked. "Boy, that is a huge amount of money. Wow, I would love to see a check with that many zeros. Jeepers, that is just crazy money." By now he had worked himself into a frenzy and was practically drooling. He beseeched me to see the check. The look in his eyes frightened me. I felt like I had won the lottery, and I was about to be bumped off and rolled for the ticket. I convinced myself that was crazy. I pulled the check out of the envelope and showed it to Pete. I could see in his face that money represented the answer to all his problems, and any doubt in himself he might harbor. It also fueled a type of jealousy that moved him to action. Pete made the largest sale the firm had ever seen a few months later. He disappeared after he got his commission check. Everyone assumed he had quit to work with another competitor. I later learned that Pete was a hopeless cocaine addict.

THE 30 YEAR PAYCHECK

Two summers after moving to Chicago, I was making more money than anyone (even the NY bankers) I knew from my graduating class. But that was about to change radically. Many of my classmates were just graduating from Law School, or entering their rotations as doctors, with huge debt loads but the promise of heinous future incomes. One such classmate was Matt. He had just finished UNC Law and had landed a consulting job with a high-tech firm. He bounced around from city to city with his new job, and it was only a matter of time before he made it to Chicago. It was great to see him, but I will never forget his departure. We had had lunch together near my office and I was seeing him off on the train platform. He was heading to O'Hare and I was going back to work. Somehow we got talking about salaries and I confided in him how much money I had made the year before. Matt is a sharp guy and rarely looks flustered, let alone dumbfounded. His face registered both as the L doors closed and his train left.

Communicate was growing too. We moved the business office function into a renovated warehouse on Clybourne Street. The city often forgot to plow there, as it dead ended into Cabrini Green. I carried a snow shovel in my car to get me in and out of parallel parking spots on the street. There were a lot of vacant buildings and a late night club, where young adults dropped acid and danced all night. At the new office, I was finally awarded a proper cube. Amos and Xavier had offices, with doors! We had sales meetings in a big glass enclosed conference room. I have to say, I actually missed sitting at a long bench, throwing paper wads at my friends and listening in on every conversation. The new environment seemed sterile. It seemed more about avoiding risk than making the next big thing happen.

When you are in your early twenty's, four years seems like an eternity. After all, in four years I went from being a high school graduate to being a college graduate, with an entirely new set of friends and a new world view. Four years in a hardened sales environment like Communicate was equally transformative. I had also entered adulthood in many other ways. I was married to a wonderful woman I had met at Duke and I single-handedly put her through Northwestern Law School on my sales commissions.

One day, I found myself buried in deep traffic on the Eisenhower Expressway daydreaming about my wife's impending graduation. I could not wait for her to start earning money. Each month was a struggle anew. My actual salary had not risen above the initial "poverty level" offer. However, I was making a pile of cash in commissions each month and running like a madman from Gary, Indiana, to Elgin, to Winnetka and through every nook and cranny Chicago had to offer. I cannot say it was ever dull, but it did become routine. It started to feel like a chore using the various 'close lines' I had learned from Zig on the next set of unsuspecting buyers. I felt I helped many of them enormously with our products, but others I wasn't quite so sure.

One such case was a large sewing machine part manufacturer on the southwest side of town. I cold called Flo Perk for a year, and developed a relationship with her over the phone. When I first called her, the company was not in the market for a new phone system, but she asked me to keep her on my list. I did, and now I was going to see her regularly.

THE 30 YEAR PAYCHECK

Their office was sandwiched between the Stephenson Expressway and the vast rail yards that moved freight in and out of the city. Flo was a middle aged woman, with kids not much younger than I, and I could see from the first day she was looking for a friend. She steeped me in her company's lore and explained how sewing at home was not a dying art as so many considered. Sure, they were the last of their kind in that industry, but they controlled nearly 100% of the market share for sewing machine parts. Their revenues continued to increase, and they took more and more calls each year. They needed a big new phone system and Flo wanted to buy it from me. Eventually, she evaluated several companies and then came back to me asking for my 'best and final'. Rarely was I in a position like this so I asked her where I needed to be. Surprisingly, she told me. She just liked me. She wanted to do business with me.

On the day she signed the contract I drank black coffee for the first time in my life with her out of small Styrofoam cups. I figured I would emulate Flo. But my stomach started to burn and my mind was racing. Then I thought about the conversation my wife and I were having about leaving Chicago after she graduated. I felt that the relationship I had with Flo was not real and was built on a large stack of false premises. Is it all right to let other people like you and reward you for what they imagine you to be and not what you really are? I wanted out of sales. I wasn't sure I could take it anymore. It wasn't the grind-- that part was fun. And it wasn't the stigma of telling people I was a salesperson (after all 10% of our GDP is derived from salespeople). I just felt like I was losing the person I was and it didn't feel right. Give me a lower paying desk job in a museum, I thought. Shoot, I would work in food service. That always sounded like fun, though I had never been a waiter like so many other people I knew.

I felt broken-hearted, as if Flo represented all the customer relationships I had made over those years. But this wasn't me. I wasn't actually a sales person. Flo gave me a hug and got teary when I told her I was quitting. I turned and walked out, I never looked back. I had Laurie's graduation party to plan, and I was happy to lay down this burden. I had saved more than $50K and no one was going to tell me what to do. Really, no one begrudged me. After all, my wife had found a job in St Paul, Minnesota.

When I finally told Amos I was leaving and my last day would be May 1st, it engendered quite a different reaction than I anticipated. He blankly stared at me, and asked me to repeat the date. "May 1st," I said. He wrote it down and went back to his spread sheet. I stood in the doorway. He hadn't asked me to sit down. He rarely did. Allowing someone to sit in your office, in Amos's mind, meant that at least five minutes in your day were about to be lost. So, I paused in the doorway and looked at the side of his head. For me it seemed like I lingered for an hour, but it was probably twenty seconds. He never looked up. I had been with him for four years. I thought about how proudly he introduced me as his 'college hire from Duke'. Now his head was filled with other problems. The company had swelled to 70 employees, and the walls were closing in. Making each month profitable and keeping the lights on was hard with a bloated payroll. He needed outside investment to protect this business he had nurtured. I may have felt I was pivotal to his success, but I didn't amount to much in his mind at that moment.

Chapter 5

Minnesota in three acts:
Act One

The sun streams into my eyes as it disappears into the west. It is 9.49 pm on the dashboard clock of the Ryder truck. The leaves are hardly on the trees, and the tall pines barely conceal the truck as we wend our way north toward Eau Claire, Wisconsin on Interstate 94. Laurie's job clerking for a Minnesota Court of Appeals judge doesn't start until August. In the meantime, she needs to study for, and pass, the Minnesota State Bar Exam. I have a wad of money in my pocket and no intention of working. We spend the first month in our new apartment visiting the Twin Cities as tourists would, and taking many camping trips around the state. Minnesota was literally and figuratively a breath of fresh air to us. I still fantasized about settling down and writing the great American novel as my wife used her clerkship to spring-board to a high paying corporate law job. With no law school or college debts, we would quickly outpace other fledgling lawyers in wealth. Our goal was simple. We wanted a small house with some land. I considered becoming a small-time gentleman farmer. I had no idea at all what that would entail. All I knew was that, compared to Illinois, land had to be cheaper in Minnesota. But for now, Laurie buckles down and studies. Unemployed and loving it, I read books, send taunting postcards to the working stiffs, and sit on the couch. But I become restless. I insist on doing things around the apartment that are annoying to someone studying for an exam. After a week of such disturbances it is clear that I need something to do. Fine, but it is not going to be a new career. At twenty-five, I am done with that nonsense. I apply for jobs at a liquor store and a bagel chain. The bagel chain calls back first, and my wish comes true. I am employed in food service. But I am a disaster from the very beginning. My status as the new guy ensures the worst hours and jobs possible. I spend long periods of times scalding myself with hot water, washing dishes that in my opinion the baker frivolously made filthy. My work is judged as 'poor' by my nineteen year old crew chief Nancy, who has been working there for a year now since she graduated from high school. She rules with an iron fist. She is stealing from the cashbox, and orchestrates a fake heist of the establishment with her boyfriend. It is interesting to note that the police detect something amiss in her story, investigate more closely, and bust her.

The good news was that I was away from the house and making a little money while my wife studied. The bad news was I found myself complaining about work when I was at home. I was supposed to be doing this for fun, but somehow it had become stressful. The more I thought about it, the more I wondered why I was putting myself through the ringer. If I was going to work, why not get a 'real' job with a 'real' salary, and a boss who at least had a college education. So much for food service. I was done in three months. On my wife's first day in the new court building on Constitution Drive, I made my first ever rush hour commute to Minneapolis for an interview.

Trying to figure out where to work was not difficult. I had tried a radical change and the results and the pay could not have been worse. No matter that my stint in food services was supposed to be fun, an 'un-job', and something to kill time. The lesson had been simple enough. Working is not fun. So, as long as you are working, get paid as much as possible. Logically speaking, the best bet to get the most money was a job where I had experience. Selling technology made a lot of sense. I had no friends or colleagues in Minnesota, so I went back to the well. I called up my uncle in Philly who had given me the internship at To-talCom and asked him if he knew anyone in Minnesota. It just so happened that he did.

The interview and eventual hiring is a blur now, but I was surprised that I had to take a test on selling and what I knew about technology. The one question I remembered from the test is "You have a choice of fixing one customer's problem or selling something new to another client, which one do you do?" 'Well,' I thought, 'that is an interesting dilemma. What would Amos Maraisons do? Both, I guess.' I tried to answer that way. The exam was oral. The interrogator made me choose. So I did. This was vexing to me. I had to make a binary decision. We make decisions like this every day, but usually in an enormous hierarchy of choices that allows black and white to skid quickly into gray. This was my first hint that working in a large corporation was going to be a very different affair. The next clue was the amount of time it took for me to get my offer letter. Before following up, I waited a week longer than the hiring manager told me it would take. The manager said she would check into it with Danny in Human Resources. Three days later, I had the letter in my mailbox.

In comparison to the job at the bagel joint, the pay was princely. It was actually ridiculous in comparison. How could my time be worth this much more to TotalCom? Obviously, they were paying for the experience and track record I had cobbled together on the mean streets of Chicago. But this track record did nothing for me at the bagel joint. I could not even call myself a competent employee there. What was I about to get myself into? The bagel joint job was just a job, not a career. I realized I had to work for the rest of my life, but I felt like I had learned a valuable lesson in Chicago. Work takes a lot of time and energy and before stepping into something new, isn't it worthwhile to assess if it was something I was passionate about? My round brain was being shoved into another square hole at TotalCom. The company needed account managers to work with customers in a new Mid-Markets segment and were willing to pay a market rate. That was the transaction. They didn't want me or my specific skills. TotalCom was willing to make a trade: money for what it said on my resume. More simply put, the hiring manager was being tasked with getting the bodies to fill the desired headcount allotted. Was I willing to make that trade? I had no idea what I really wanted to do. I had spent most of the past four years hustling to make money. Something inside me missed that rat race. Maybe I had just grown accustomed to it. My new base salary was double what I made at Communicate. That sounded good. I would get paid well regardless of what I sold. When I asked about the commission plan,

I found it to be unintelligible in comparison to the '10% plan' from Communicate. Maybe it was greed, or maybe I let go of the prospect of finding my passion at twenty-five. I took the job and reported to work on the last day of August, 1994.

Here is how the first day went. Danny, the human resources guy, meets me at the door and lets me in. He seems nervous. He escorts me to a cubicle by the windows overlooking a parking lot. On a wall behind the parking lot is a huge mural of a musical score. He hurriedly removes some boxes from my space and places them by the wall. He tells me there is another 'new hire' starting that day, and once she arrives he will come get me and talk to us both. I sit down in my new environs. It is dirty from use. I wait a half hour, at the ready for Danny to appear. It is apparent he is not coming back soon. Bored, I look through the drawers and cabinets, trying to get a bead on the person who had inhabited this space before me. I find some files labeled with customer names I have never heard of. A broken pair of green rimmed women's sunglasses, pens and paperclips, a few spare pennies and an empty pack of gum round out the contents of one of the drawers. Then I find a business card. Cathy L., TotalCom Account Executive. I wonder where she is. I look at my watch. The clock shows 10:45 am.

Before I can get upset about the colossal waste of time, Danny rounds the corner. He is smiling and has Regina in tow. Regina is about my age, and she is dressed in a smart blue suit and uncomfortable shoes. As she shakes my hand, I sense some annoyance in her voice and immediately take it personally. It is funny how often we believe people are mad at us when they are really angry about something else entirely.

For example, I remember visiting Florida and looking up a couple who were dear friends of ours in Chicago. Something seemed odd. At first, they didn't invite us over and eventually did so only after first meeting at a local park. I wracked my brain that night trying to imagine how we had slighted either of them in the past year-- Facebook or otherwise. Soon after our visit I learned they were getting divorced.

Danny seems much calmer now and announces that he is going to take us on a tour of the building. As we board the elevator, Danny explains that only half the building is occupied by TotalCom. He courteously says hello to a group of people piling off the elevator with half-filled paper coffee cups. Danny presses a down button and we descend from the seventh floor to the third. In Minneapolis, the second level is a Skyway access and rarely has any office space. On the third floor, when the doors open we are immediately hit by a cloud of cigarette smoke. Danny explains that this floor has the phone switch rooms and the 'break' rooms. We walk into a room the size of a school cafeteria. The center is open and completely empty, like it is being prepared for a school dance. Along one side there is a refrigerator, sink and some vending machines. The rest of the room is lined with beat up furniture, arranged in short combinations to create make-shift sofas and couches. In one such combo, a bearded guy with a Van Halen tee shirt, jeans and a stubbly beard is fast asleep. There is only one other person in the room. She is middle-aged and extremely overweight. She sits reading a paperback that has a horse with flowing mane on the cover. Danny explains, sotto voce, that there are twenty-four hour operations in the building and that union rules allow people to take certain liberties in the break room. We round the bend and open a large oak door. The room is packed with people smoking. The atmosphere is a shade of dull yellow. Regina suddenly brightens up and calls out to a very fit but aging woman in a similar blue suit. "Hiya Rox!"

Regina tells us that Rox is a friend of her mom's and she is the one who told her about this job. Rox is talking to a male version of herself and both of them are holding cigarettes that are burned down right to the nub. Danny asks how everyone's weekend was, and we politely duck back into the large room, and then return to the elevator.

We rise to the fourth floor. This is where the Regional Vice President sits. Her offices are palatial if not a bit dark and sterile. A woman named Candy greets us. When Danny makes it clear he intends to introduce us, Candy sourly rises and walks over to an enormous door in the corner behind her reception pad. She peers in as if she smells a dead animal in the vicinity, and then she closes the door. She is much more pleasant after that. She welcomes us and explains to Regina and me that she is Loni's secretary. Suddenly, the big door swings open fifteen inches, and a lanky woman with a white shirt that makes her short neck look even shorter, peers out. Her bulging eyes deliberately miss ours, and she asks Candy to come in and see her "real quick" in a pleasant yet urgent tone. Candy drops our conversation like a scalding piece of metal, and obeys. I get the impression I won't be spending too much time on the fourth floor. Our tour of the building then picks up. We quickly visit floor five (operations), floor six (call center), and floor eight (small business sales). On these floors, Danny makes sure to press the button so we can look out and behold the floor's lobby in all its repetitive grandness.

Then we move on. By the time we get to the twelfth floor, I am unable to remember anything about the other floors and I wrack my brain to remember what floor I work on. I figure if I get off on the wrong floor I am in big trouble unless it is the break room on floor three. They all look exactly alike down to the carpeting and pictures on the wall.

After we return to Danny's office, he briefs us on how to use the voice mail system to check messages. This is no problem for me. I have been selling voice mail systems for four years, for crying out loud. After that Danny starts reading to us from a print-out detailing the holidays we have for the year. "We have Thanksgiving, Christmas, New Year's...." On one hand it seems surreal that we are listening to this list. But, on the other hand, we have a lot of days off. At Communicate, you were expected to work hard enough to make the money you desired. You could take any day off you wanted, but it meant one less day to sell. The higher salaries at the larger company necessitated a strict delineation of what days we all worked versus the days we did not.

Danny suggests we take a lunch break and meet up again afterwards. He rises, looks at his watch, grabs his gym bag and heads for the elevator. Regina and I decide to get a slice of pizza in the Skyway and chit chat. We get back to Danny's office a few minutes after 1pm. Danny comes racing back to his office at 1:25 with his hair still a little wet. 'He just went and worked out over lunch,' I think to myself. So this is how it is done in big companies. It seemed very civilized to me. Another part of me was chomping at the bit to get busy and start doing something. All the people on our floor I met that morning seem to be working in slow motion. They are so quiet, too. It is hard to believe this is a sales floor. Maybe everyone is out with their customers. Who knows?

Danny is out of breath and looking nervous, but he brightens up when he sees Lorna walking toward his office. Lorna is a sales manager and she looks old enough to be my mom. She wants to know all about Regina and me. After she hears our brief bio's, she begins to talk about TotalCom and TotalCom culture. Her words are steeped in mystery and pride. After a few minutes of hearing about the founding fathers of TotalCom, she turns to us and asks, "Do you want to be promoted someday?" We both nod. She retorts, "Do you plan to go to business school?" Regina and I immediately, and with conviction, answer differently.

You will recall my promise to never, ever, ever, ever go to school again that I had made about five years ago? I stick to my guns. Lorna: "Well, you will never be promoted then." Promoted? I was still trying to figure out what the hell they wanted us to do.

Poor Danny had no idea what to do with us. TotalCom had hired us, but the branch manager did not know what teams we should be on or what customers we should support. In fact, our charge would eventually become to find our own customers via cold calling. So we sat for weeks in our cubes without a laptop or anything to do. Over time I learned that Danny had flunked out of the sales ranks, and was given the branch human resources title. Years later, after he took a golden parachute package from TotalCom, he found another human resources job at a large auto dealership in town. A huge scandal broke out there over sexual harassment in the office. As the story unfolded in the St Paul Pioneer Press, I pitied Danny. There was no way he was prepared to handle a situation like that. He could barely carry on a conversation with two new hires.

Anyway, Lorna couldn't and wouldn't let it go. In the end, I agreed she was right about the MBA, if only to get her to drop it and move on. Lorna was in charge of the new and hip 'data services' team which was selling a new product at outrageous prices. My ears perked up. I had sold some of these new services at Communicate via our Illinois Bell relationship and it was a much more interesting sale than a phone system.

When I got back to my desk, my message light was on. I deftly dialed-in to see who could have possibly even known I was there. I had not yet even given my number to my wife. The message was a minute and a half of a woman screaming obscenities. 'That's interesting', I thought. I moved on figuring it must have been a wrong number.

After a week of sitting around doing nothing, I was going crazy. I tried to convince myself how great it was that I was being paid to do nothing, but it soon seemed like a prison sentence. Regina complained to her friend Rox and the next week, after their leadership team meeting, Danny came by to speak with us. "We want you two to research potential new customers," he said. Our job was to go to the library (remember this is pre-Internet days) and look for potential companies to call on that were not already in one of our databases. Finding businesses was a snap. Figuring out our internal systems was the hard part. The system was finicky. "ABC Company" could be loaded "abc company" or "A.B.C Company" or "ABC Company Inc." Finding matches was extremely difficult. Danny promised us we could keep any customers we found. At this rate we wouldn't find any that we could say with certainty were not in our database. We would find out how many times we failed at this exercise in the coming months.

One day when we returned from the library I had another voice mail message. This time it was a customer. The message was for Cathy even though my "This is me" greeting was on the line. "Cathy, long time, no talk. Hope you are well. We need to disconnect some services. Please give us a call..." It gradually occurred to me that I had Cathy's old phone number. But it wasn't until I met the Hedgehog that I fully understood it all...including the obscene screams.

I asked Danny to come to my desk so I could play the customer message. He knew just what to do. He disappeared around the corner and returned with a woman who reminded me of a younger version of my grandmother. This was the Hedgehog. Her face was severely painted over: Ruby red lips, sky blue eye shadow and jet black eyelashes and eyebrows. She limply shook my hand and acted as though she needed a napkin to get my cooties off her. She asked to hear the message, and she dutifully scribbled down some of the details. She instructed me to then delete it.

The Hedgehog would eventually become my manager, but that was still a few months off. The corporate organization for Mid-Markets was new, but it didn't feel that way. TotalCom had restructured, and a large number of people who were formerly with business sales in support roles were moved into a direct selling role in this new Mid-Market venture. It seemed that a Big Eight consultancy had advised TotalCom it was missing the boat in a revival in US businesses that was occurring in this middle market, but both the consultancies and TotalCom were late getting into the game. Better late than never. I had been riding the tide of this shift at Communicate for the past four years in Chicago.

A newly minted Sales VP named Ricky was brought in to our office. He was a superstar, full of energy and the knowledge of how to breed success. He came from an acquisition TotalCom had made and later sold for pennies on the dollar. Ricky brought one salesperson with him to the new job. His name was Tran and he worked for Lorna. He was an entrepreneur working both sides of the door. He had a job at TotalCom, but he also owned a small business consulting clients looking to install data communications. He was also getting involved with a brand new technology-- the Internet.

Ricky was known for his flashy style. In his leadership meetings he always showed a picture of his children as the opening slide. This brought a sense of purpose and heart and you couldn't help but like him. Years later, when he had been promoted to a new job in New York, I noticed other TotalCom leaders were adopting his idea with varying success. Once, I bumped into Ricky at a conference in Los Angeles and mentioned that copying was the highest form of flattery. He didn't even hear me. His eyes were roaming the convention center floor, and he only had stopped to chat with me so he could take stock of the next conversation he wanted to have. Ricky bounced around to many telecom carriers after that, always jumping for a shinier title or a little more ka-ching. Last I heard he was back with a firm in Minneapolis ostensibly doing the same thing he had always done except for more money. I suppose it was what he was best at, but I am not sure his leadership skills are any different now than they were twenty years ago. I heard he had recently hired a ringer from his previous company to help improve his new firm's numbers in Minneapolis. Some things never change.

Ricky was very approachable and even I could get time with him to talk about my accounts. He had a palatial corner office behind the secretarial pool. His secretary liked him and she was really laid back.

Another character in the office was Jimmy Luzinski. He had been a salesperson, but recently applied for the role of IT manager for the new sales group and, without so much as a degree in computer science, got the job. Jimmy was the ultimate laggard and made Danny look like a busy bee. Jimmy had rolled out new Microsoft software when I first arrived and had discovered the game of Solitaire embedded in the new version. Jimmy was instantly hooked. He had a hard time answering his phone or doing much of anything else. My cube was very close to his, and because I was going into my third month without assigned accounts or duties, I kept a pretty close eye on him. Like any good addict, he shared his passion with the management staff. One by one, he converted the entire management team into Solitaire fiends.

I was surprised to find Ricky sucked in by this behavior, but a few months later when I walked over to his office he was staring at his screen clicking his mouse. "Just a minute. I need to finish up this email" he said to me. It was a particularly dreary day in Minneapolis and the reflection of his screen on the window behind him was in plain view to me. He deftly played his cards and won the round of Solitaire. I felt a sense of accomplishment for him and smiled. You see, by then I too had become an office Solitaire junky. Jimmy couldn't hide it from me and I asked him too many questions. Productivity was probably at an all-time low thanks to Jimmy Luzinski.

It seemed like the new sales team had marketing dollars, and headquarters had big plans to spend that dough. Other companies were eating our proverbial lunch and we wanted to win those customers back. More importantly, we did not want to lose any more. Tran Nugyen, Ricky's ace seller acquainted me with the concept of 'Fear Uncertainty and Doubt' (or the F.U.D. factor) when selling to a client. Basically, the idea is quite simple. Prey on your customers' fears, their fear of change and failure, to get them to do what you wanted. This was utterly foreign to me. My previous four years were about eliciting change from the status quo, and finding new ideas for business to better serve customers and make employees more efficient. It seemed to me that the F.U.D. factor cut both ways. Tran assured me it was the fastest way to make money at TotalCom. Later, I had to agree. But as I watched TotalCom's market share decrease from one year to the next, I wasn't quite sure this was the best approach for a viable long term business to expand-- let alone maintain revenues.

It appeared that the Marketing team liked the F.U.D. factor too. They started a campaign called "For Your Business' Life". The intent was to paint TotalCom as the right partner if you hoped to remain in business. Fifteen years later, this new-fangled slogan and the letter explaining the campaign's importance, signed by Loni , the sales VP on the fourth floor, still proudly hangs on her wall.

Minnesota in three acts: Act One

Marketing decided that each customer should get a welcome package explaining why TotalCom protected its business better than other companies, especially the new competitors in the market. The welcome package consisted of a box with blue lettering "For Your Business' Life" and included the letter from Loni, a few brochures and a pack of Lifesavers candy. Because Mid-Markets was going after a big new swath of customers, we had thousands of boxes to hand out. At least that is what our marketing department thought. Marketing sent all the boxes in one shipment to our floor. If you do the math on thousands of shoebox size boxes packed into larger cardboard boxes at twenty-five per large box, you can quickly see our dilemma. Every bit of useable space on the seventh floor was overloaded with boxes of boxes that consisted of five sheets of paper and a package of Lifesavers. You could hardly make your way to the bathroom without tripping over them. Ricky sent out the alarm to get the boxes out to customers, but there is only so much a team of 30 can do to chip away at so many boxes of boxes. At the time, I was blown away by the waste. The shipping costs alone to move this much air had to be staggering. If the small boxes were flattened, all of this could have been shipped in a tenth of the packaging. After two months, there were still a staggering number of boxes unopened. One morning, I came in to find Jimmy at his cube opening the boxes one by one with a box cutter. What was he up to? I kept quiet and watched him work. As if he were cleaning a fish, he would open each smaller box, remove the candy, and drop it into a now overflowing file drawer. He then moved on to another box. I don't think I saw Jimmy without a lifesaver in his mouth for the next year. I am sure his dentist reaped the biggest reward.

Ultimately things ended badly for Jimmy. A year or so later, another new sales segment was started for 'low share' accounts. This was an Elysian Fields for sales people. The compensation plan paid out for taking a customer who mainly did business with our competition to lunch or introducing him to our Sales VP. Almost everything about this group didn't make sense from the outset. Everyone wanted to work there. Jimmy quickly applied to be their IT person. He then moved up-market from Lifesavers and got accused of selling used computer equipment that he had upgraded for the group. He was not convicted because there was not enough evidence. However, TotalCom did move him to Chicago and put him in a sales support role helping with custom pricing. This maneuver was called putting someone in the 'penalty box.' Instead of firing Jimmy, he was just moved to a place where he could not cause any more damage and his career would stall. I bumped into him years later when I was a sales manager. But, something had changed. When I realized it was him, I lit up. He did just the opposite. I made a crack about the Lifesavers that was met with a short stifled chuckle. It was as if a gene had been removed from his DNA. It could be he felt embarrassed by where his career had led him, but I think I reminded him of his self-inflicted prison sentence at TotalCom. I had a strange inkling that if he could leave the company he would. The problem was he couldn't. He was trapped by fear and had forgotten how to get up and walk away.

Minnesota in three acts: Act One

Those early years, I straddled a group of people who began working for TotalCom when it was a monopoly. What did it mean to be in sales when no one else sold the services you had and everybody needed them? It meant you reacted each day to what came your way, and then took whatever monetary reward you were given. Excess money was literally burned by the company at the end of the year by flying entire divisions to exotic locations, like Cleveland, for the purpose of a business meeting followed by heavy drinking. My sales VP Loni used to say, "If you didn't work in this place during the monopoly years, you haven't lived." When I heard Jimmy on the phone, or witnessed any number of the stories I will share in the upcoming pages, I am not so sure if that was truly 'living' or just some proxy thereof. Regina and I were the new kids, and were in absolute shock at what we saw each day. Miles kept a bottle of booze in his desk drawer. Denny took a severe tongue lashing for expensing a trip to a striptease club with his customer, but no one was taking as much advantage of the situation as Tran.

Tran was making money coming and going in what was clearly a conflict of interest in three directions. But, to me, he seemed like the only person truly concerned with business and money. He was helping Ricky crush his branch quota for new data services and he had become my idol. I was enamored by the Internet, and believed it could solve everyone's problems. Tran seemed to understand this too, along with his group of high-tech employees who hung out in a cheap office suite in Bloomington, tinkering around with avatars and virtual reality...this was 1995, people! I started to bring Tran out to see all of my customers.

He represented big ideas. He stuttered and spoke with a thick accent, but he had a way of getting people's interest.

My boss, the Hedgehog, hated Tran. When I started growing my hair out, and hanging around Tran I could see it made her nervous. One day, the book *Dress to Impress* was found in my chair. During my one-on-one with her, she told me how it was: "At TotalCom we wear suits each day. And a tie." She told me the camel hair sport coat I wore the day before was a 'little too casual' for midweek. At the time, it was the most expensive piece of clothing I owned. She danced around the topic of my hair which was slowly reaching the length of a 'bob', but I assume she had lived through the 1970's and felt she couldn't quite broach the topic. Either way, I wasn't fitting in around there and she needed to act quickly to preserve corporate culture. I told her I wanted to sell the data products and felt the Internet was going to be huge. Now there is a prediction! She reminded me that I had been "in title" less than a year and I needed to prove myself like others on the team had before I could do something new. "Like who?" I said.

"Tom," she replied.

Tom was a quiet, balding guy about 30 years old. His cube was closest to the elevator and so, for him, the best spot in the house. He rarely came into the office, but never missed a team event or team meeting. His module was loaded with winners by the Hedgehog's design. At the time, we were being paid 7% of the monthly committed value of a contract if the customer signed a three year deal. TotalCom was trying to incent sales teams to keep customers locked in. Meanwhile, the market was in a steep decline. Tom had figured out this game to perfection.

Each year he would create new three year contracts for each of his large customers.

He had 'the talk' with each of them:

"You see Ms. Corporate Buyer, the market has changed and prices are going down. If you sign a three year contract you are locked-in in the event the market changes. And you will get the best price from Total-Com today. I will come back next December and will re-contract you for a new 3 year agreement if prices keep going down."

It was brilliant. Buyers never needed to shop, and saved their business money each year. Meanwhile, the biggest bonuses were paid in January when TotalCom realized it had spent another year losing share and revenue, and kickers were often paid out to turn the tide. On January second of each year, Tom rode around town and picked up contracts. He closed the quota for 'retaining' business for the year and made a fortune in the process.

The sales kick-off was held in a swank new Hilton hotel each year in March. Tom was brought up on stage each year to receive an over-sized check. He then stood behind it with Loni and Ricky to have his photo taken. The checks were for $30,000, $40,000 or even $50,000. I sat incredulous. My module contained no one spending more than a few thousand dollars with TotalCom each month. Most of them were in business suffering from one economic crisis or another. And I had to compete with actual competitors, who were offering prices we could not match. I watched as business walked away.

THE 30 YEAR PAYCHECK

The Hedgehog was furious with me for my customer's actions. How could I let them leave TotalCom? How could I let this happen? Why couldn't I be more like Tom? A sour-grapes excuse would not work. Quoth the Hedgehog: "You will never get into the Data/Internet division at TotalCom if you don't make your quota."

I gave it some thought. I had tried to play the game like Tom, but I realized it was time to go back into Communicate-mode. I wanted that Internet job, so I went on the offensive.

I decided to look for customers who were with other carriers already. We were permitted to get better pricing and even ask for custom deals if we were beating out a competitor and the revenue was new to Total-Com. I tried to find the companies who were friendliest with us. There was one high-tech firm where the buyer had long hair and never wore shoes. He became my first success. Then there was a motherly-like woman who had two small adopted daughters from China and worked for a large ice cream restaurant chain. She became enamored with me, and it was Flo Perk all over again. I wrested some basketball tickets from VP Loni to entertain her. This was a huge coup orchestrated in no small way by Ricky. The Timberwolves were a new NBA franchise and Loni loved basketball. Or, should I say, her children loved basketball. The TotalCom tickets were right behind the visitor's bench.

Several weeks before, a guy on my team named Mike had asked for the tickets to take his potato chip manufacturer client who was on the fence about working with TotalCom. The Hedgehog took the request up the chain and came back with the bad news that they were taken. Later that day, the potato chip maker decided to go with a competitor.

Minnesota in three acts: Act One

Afterward, Mike and I went out to Runyon's bar to drown his sorrows. We stayed late enough that the game came on TV. A close up of the visiting team during the introductions provided a clear view of Loni and her two sons eating popcorn and yucking it up behind the bench. Mike just shook his head.

Anyway, this time I got the tickets. However, things were to go very bad for me at the game because of Mike. He had spent a lot of time in the bar since that potato chip loss. Besides alcohol, Mike also loved basketball. We arranged that he would buy the cheapest ticket at the Target Center and then come down to the TotalCom seats after half-time. My customer was bringing her two daughters and we reasoned that they may want to go home by then and Mike and I could enjoy the game after they left. Mike had been drinking a lot of beer in the balcony during the first half. The game was close and my customer and her daughters were not leaving early. During the half-time Mike sauntered down the steep concrete stairs to our row with a thirty ounce beer in his hand. I can still see him now. My customer sat on the aisle, I sat four seats deep, and my customer's daughters sat between us. Just as I looked over at Mike, he stumbled and slipped. The contents of his still full thirty ounce beer landed in my clients lap. She gasped for air upon feeling the cold liquid. Mike apologized profusely and quickly slipped away. She was not pleased. She asked me if I knew the guy or had ever seen him before. I felt like I was back in the TotalCom job interview questionnaire. A binary answer was required of me. Sure, I knew him, but what would be her opinion of me if I admitted it? I looked her directly in the eye and said, "I don't know him."

The fates frowned on me after that. The new services we were installing for the ice cream chain client were ordered incorrectly and the initial cut to the new system did not work. Furthermore, I did not come to the cutover and my client spent the whole night troubleshooting with the TotalCom technicians. She wanted me off the account and told the Hedgehog as much. The Hedgehog was all too happy to do this. However, it worked out well because I was paid for the sale and did not have to support it.

Additionally, my boss agreed to give Lorna my name as a candidate for a new Internet sales person. Tran needed help. He was selling like crazy and he told Ricky he needed a junior salesperson to mop up after him. I got a subscription to 'Wired Magazine' to improve my chances, and started reading a book on data communications. I was going to be tested and needed to pass in order to get the job. I also started spending more time with Tran.

My hair grew by the micro-meter and I spent a day at the Minnesota State Fair that September handing out software disks that enabled people to sign up for our services over the Internet. High tech! Tran had purchased hundreds of little wooden dowels that we taped to the box that held the software CD. At the Minnesota state fair, a lot of food is sold 'on a stick' so you can walk with it. Tran built a huge sign that read 'software on a stick'. The thing I didn't know was that he was being paid a twenty dollars in commission for each CD we gave away. He even had the gall to invite a product manager from TotalCom to come out to the event. She was a young woman from New York in a marketing director role. She watched her product move like hotcakes and couldn't have been happier. That evening, Tran suggested we grab dinner and drinks on Nicollett Island. He ordered Carpaccio, lobster and bottle after bottle of wine. The whole meal had to have cost several hundred dollars. The marketing manager grabbed the bill and insisted on paying. Tran did not refuse and certainly I did not either. We had given away CD's, earned Tran thousands of dollars and the only payment for me was a free meal on TotalCom's tab. As I made my way home, I could not wrap my head around it. How was Tran able to be paid like a prince and loved by everyone when in reality all we had done that day was spend TotalCom's money? The take rate for those CD's to come out of the box was well under 1%. At the time AOL was sending CD's as junk mail to every living American in order to flummox Wall Street with the sheer numbers of subscribers. At our next sales meeting, Ricky heralded Tran's selling as inventive and wonderful. After all, Ricky's ship was rising on the results that Tran was turning in. In Tran's defense, he was just taking advantage of a compensation plan built by people who didn't understand the Internet market to begin with. While we were at the fair, Tran excused himself and went to various radio stations which were broadcasting live. He had another idea. What if radio were broadcasted over the Internet? There is no mistake that Tran was incredibly smart and well ahead of his time. This idea eventually took off as a way for radio stations to reach audiences beyond the reach of their airways. But Tran was also impatient and a risk-taker. When he could not get existing stations to bite on the idea, he invested in a company called Net Tunes, sold them insane amounts of TotalCom services and promptly watched the rocket go up and fall back to earth in a fiery blaze. His idea was ten years too early.

Tran's impatience hit a zenith a few years later. His company had become a TotalCom agent and made commission on selling TotalCom products. But he still worked for TotalCom and funneled all his business through his company. That way, he was paid as an agent and as a salesperson. To make it more bizarre, he set up a virtual store on the seventh floor. He offered to help other sales people with their deals and if help was not enough, he got the managers to pressure their teams to work with his firm. He accomplished this by elaborate 'profit sharing' incentives. This was the new, and much more powerful game of 'Solitaire' released on the middle managers with doors to their offices. Amazingly, this incredible conflict-of-interest was not what finally brought him down. He continued like this for years as the sales center improbably beat its quotas year after year. Tran was working with more advanced technological solutions by now, and his firm was pioneering the use advanced software, and other concepts to augment the TotalCom Internet services. Through his technical discussions with TotalCom engineers, he learned of an impending purchase of a small technology firm. The dotcom bubble was inflating and fleecing large firms like TotalCom of its cash even faster than market share was shrinking to new entrepreneurs. Tran cashed in on Wall Street on the deal. He made the mistake of telling others in his company and some higher level local employees at TotalCom. Insider trading was big business at that time as the world cranked out mergers and acquisitions and start-ups at an incredible clip. I read in the newspaper that he had settled with the FTC by paying a hefty fine. Last I heard, he was still running his business after departing from TotalCom.

Tran had crossed over the line, and he met the consequences of doing so, but up until that point, I watched him with astonishment. He operated in a very different way than most of the people I was now working with. I watched salespeople ground to dust trying to get competitive pricing, or get an offer to a perspective client before they re-signed with a competitor. Installation of new services always takes longer than expected, and frequently there was pressure from customers as the sales team is squeezed up against the wall of TotalCom bureaucracy. Somehow, Tran operated outside all this. He seemed to constantly fly at a higher altitude than any of the aforementioned hazards. Whenever he faced resistance from others, he was so far out of reach that any attempt to slow him down was rarely more than specious. Additionally, his status with Ricky often made any attempt to critique him appear to be motivated by jealousy. As Tran's peers one by one dropped away for not making their sales quotas, the buzz was that he was dangerous.

The one salesperson who persisted was an older gentleman named Reggie. Lorna made sure Reggie did well by funneling him good accounts and leads. Much like Tom on my team, Reggie made his number in January and spent the rest of the year stirring up ill-will against Tran. The office was in a swirl and Tran moved like a jet in the direction of a newer and better world. I was prepared to be his apprentice. I just needed to pass the data test.

THE 30 YEAR PAYCHECK

I felt confident about the test, and looked forward to the transition. I was reading 'Wired Magazine' with more vigor than ever. The Internet was going to be huge and I was going to participate. Meanwhile, the Hedgehog tried to make my life as difficult as possible. She instituted bed checks, making sure I was in the office early each day and did not leave a minute before 5 pm. I instituted reading the newspaper at my desk after getting dinged twice for being late. Truth be told, the Hedgehog disappeared each day at noon for hours. I started watching her movements closely. She walked back into the office with a green Dayton's department store bag at least twice a week.

The one thing about working for TotalCom that always surprised me was how much time I had on my hands. Commission checks were not the difference between making the rent or not, and no one seemed to be in a big hurry to do anything. Even firing people was a four month ordeal that often ended with reassignment instead. This may be one of the deep seeded reasons people stay in corporate jobs as long as they do. It isn't that the job is easy or fun. It comes down to being a relatively safe place. Safety is a very basic human desire. It is much more important than success or greatness. This is why people get out of the stock market after it has fallen. They make a choice to keep their money safe and in doing so miss the inevitable upswing and growth. I noticed how often people referred to the company as 'family.' This fosters the belief that it was a safe place to spend your day in return for a living wage about which you couldn't complain. But it would never make you terribly rich either. Of course, there were those who climbed the rungs to positions of power. The pyramid shape of the command-and-control culture at TotalCom ensures that someone will make it big. But statistically speaking, you are more likely to be struck by lightning than get the nod. My last years at TotalCom, I attended five or more career seminars held by the employee resource groups. To the person, each executive attributed his or her status at least somewhat to luck or good fortune. Now they may have been being humble, or maybe they are trying to be realistic when addressing the lower blocks on the pyramid, but if you think about it the message is plain. The more you stay in place and make the safe choices, the better chance you have of promotion. Staying safe ensures you will statistically be available to win the corporate lotto that could one day give you a very large salary. However, for each rung you climb, the more important safety becomes to you. Think about it! Those who are empowered to take the biggest risks are the ones least likely to do so. As a third or fourth level employee at TotalCom, playing it safe protects a bigger and bigger salary and bonus structure and keeps you in play to win the next promotion in the corporate lottery. Pretty soon, your entire day is consumed with just keeping your job safe. This madness continues until eventually you reach officer levels where suddenly a board elected C-level team has big expectations for skills that have either withered away or have become so rusty that you have trouble understanding that paying sales people $20 per Internet CD they give away at the state fair is probably not a good long term growth strategy.

But the effect on the base of the pyramid is even more profound. Just like the lower blocks on the Great Pyramids of Giza, the base level is stressed to the maximum holding all the weight above it. And it has little or no ability to move. So why do people stay with it? Why do they continue to prop up all the weight? No matter how much stress and strain they endure, the notion of safety for themselves and their families is what keeps them in place. The company tries to keep their jobs safe in order to keep them in place to maintain and run the machine. But people under stress are not at their best. First of all, they become restrictive and defensive and feel they cannot take extra time to either innovate by trying new things or collaborate to share learning with others for fear of falling behind in their daily duties. When things get really stressful, as they did after the dotcom bust in early 2009, employees turn on each other. The old joke is that two guys in the jungle encounter a lion. The one guy bends down and laces up his running shoes. His companion says to him, "What's the use, you aren't faster than a lion." "I don't need to be faster than the lion" the runner responds, "I just need to be faster than you." I have seen real sabotage done by salespeople on other salespeople. Jealousy can rage at any time, but the worst acts of this type occur in the months leading up to a rumored lay-off. An old sales vice president of mine used to say that the best insurance against being laid off is to sell. The safety culture takes that one step further: the best insurance is really to fail a little less than others. These are destructive cultures that become life-sapping. Any upside of keeping people in line in a large company is erased by hoards of people just trying to stay in place.

The pace was so much slower at TotalCom than it was at Communicate that I hardly knew what to do. Solitaire was stealing my soul and it was not something I wanted the Hedgehog catching me doing. I couldn't imagine how bad that would be. Never mind that I knew she also was playing Solitaire during many of our reviews...the old reflection in the plate glass and months of dreary Minnesota weather behind her desk gave her away. I made a mental note to move my desk farther from the window if I ever got an office with a door.

I hated that I had more time than I knew what to do with. With a limited number of accounts and things to follow up on each day, I had too much time on my hands. I could read the entire newspaper and 'Wired Magazine' cover to cover and still have more time than I needed. I decided I should get after my life reading list. I had built this list after college when I looked at a compendium of 500 of the most famous books of all time and realized how few of them I had read. Before I got married, I was making progress knocking off many of the famous Russian novels on my weekends and evenings in Chicago. When I contemplated how much time I actually had on my hands at work, I calculated I could tackle anything the list had to offer. *Moby Dick* looked long, so I started with that.

I wait until the Hedgehog checks me in and then I head down to the break room and get cracking. I am a fixture there. I get to know the turf. I know who owns what couch and when each comes in for his nap. Sometimes, if people are talking, I move into the vestibule where the snack machines are adjacent to the smoking rooms. Many of the smokers on my floor see me. At first I feel busted, but I gradually figure they are consuming a lot of time smoking and probably don't feel guilty about that. At least I am reading and not rotting my lungs. The reading program goes swimmingly. Instead of waiting for the phone to ring, I often come back to messages and a stack of things to do that keep me busy all afternoon. Plus I am cruising through *Moby Dick*. My email prose becomes Mevillesque. "Call me....Ishmael," I conclude one voice mail to a client. For them it isn't nearly as funny. I finish Moby Dick and moved on to more and more challenging books. Eventually, I read James Joyce's *Ulysses* in tedious detail over the course of six months. My crowning achievement comes years later when I hit another lull in my work. I read all but two volumes of Gibbon's *Decline and Fall of the Roman Empire* at work. I am not overly proud of this accomplishment but I think it says a lot about what the job is doing to me. I know I have a paycheck coming, so I have no respect for the work I am supposed to be doing. There is no correlation between the pay and work anymore. I am trying, I reason. I just don't have enough to do. Looking back, I should have left the firm or found something that needed to be done then and there! There is no excuse. I would like to blame the fact that I was young, but I was reading Gibbon when I was in my late 30's.

Like the other pyramid blocks, I didn't understand that people move up the chain through intelligence and drive. I thought I just needed to keep my resume up to date and that my intrinsic value might be recognized in the corporate lotto. By reading books at work, I was exhibiting a lack of drive. As much as I hate to admit it, I once snuck into the movies in the Skyway theater with a guy named Blaine to watch a matinee. I couldn't enjoy the show. I felt guilty. But I had nothing to do at my desk, or so I reasoned. It made me mad at TotalCom. I was sitting in a nice warm room with everything I needed, but I was little more than a hamster. At any moment I could be lifted out or crushed. Sure, it was dangerous in the outside world, but there was so much to see and do, and there was an opportunity for real success. Why did I stay? The psychology is complicated and made me feel ashamed. When we had to put our accomplishments for the year on our report to our managers, I always daydreamed of including the books I had read on the job. That would be funny. Or maybe just sad.

One day, Lorna announced, with less enthusiasm than I felt appropriate, that I had passed the data/internet test. But she wanted to come on a few sales calls with me to make sure I was ready. I agreed and the next week we went to see a student loan company in St Paul. They needed some services for each of their four locations in Minnesota and they were soliciting bids. TotalCom could price this services, but was never competitive with public loan companies. This had a lot to do with the regulatory environment at that time. Lorna neglected to explain this to me. We promptly lost the business to another company. Lorna used this as an excuse to not offer me the job. She announced the next week she had hired a guy from outside the company to fill the position. I walked into her office that afternoon and closed the door and then I lost my cool. I blamed her for stringing me along. I told her I knew she didn't like the length of my hair and that no one, but no one, could ever do as well as I could in that job. I left in a huff. I always wanted to leave in a huff, and there, I did it. I left in a huff.

When I think back on the things I said to Lorna that day, I realize that most of them were really things she could not understand, let alone change. Therefore, I could have been having this discussion with myself and left her out of it. But, you can't leave in a huff in a conversation with yourself, can you? It broke the hope that she would ever help me again. It was purposeless. It made me feel good, but I got nothing from it. Lorna said if I did a stellar job on the Hedgehog's team for the next year, she would reconsider.

Another year of the Hedgehog? Too much to bear.

The next weeks were complicated. I went on a tirade about the Hedgehog with my co-workers, and could not find a single nice thing to say about her. My wife reminded me that she gave us a very pretty Christmas plate as a holiday gift.

"How did she know were weren't Jewish?" I retorted, looking for another reason to dislike her.

How long has humankind hated the boss? It is an emotional response that appears to take place at least 70% of the time. So, why do we end up working for other people if we are just going to dislike them and feel we could do a better job without their guidance? Perhaps it goes back to our need for stability. Bosses are just a single downside to the orderly control a corporate culture provides to us. The real question is, why anyone would want the boss's job? A simple reason is power and probably more money. Or maybe it is the altruistic notion that having been in sales a long time, one may have wisdom to bring to a younger generation. But that reason holds very little water in TotalCom, since imparting wisdom on a team can be done more easily by senior members of the sales team who share the same goals and pressures of a junior colleague. The manager job focuses long days on reports with higher middle managers, and a constant song and dance routine to let upper layers know that things are going as they expect. Twisting the truth into a version of reality pleasing to the next layer keeps you your job and allows you to wait for a chance to be promoted regardless of how unlikely that may be.

For a salesperson, being in a manager job appears to be a way to collect a paycheck and commission without being directly responsible for making sales. The monkeys are not on your back. Your job is to subtly remind your team each and every day that they own the monkeys. I found this out many years later when I had my chance to be the boss. Sales teams like to gang up on bosses who seem too confident and move all the work to the team. Asking for 'help' on impossible problems is one way. Telling your boss that your customer will not sign the big deal if they don't have the service installed in two days is just one way to shift the blame.

I once had a boss who went on the offensive in the blame game. He told the team that if we brought him a monkey to put on his back, he would guarantee that he would turn around and put it right back on our back. Meanwhile, he sat in his office and day-traded with his 401K retirement plan and worked the upper levels with appropriate visions of sugarplums. The sales center that year was in tough shape and we had abysmal results and a layoff. People were sick of the 'no monkey' policy. Someone on the team decided to launch a complaint to human resources. Such complaints usually fell on deaf ears unless they had direct EEOC implications, but for some reason the regional manager in Chicago took on the case. She interviewed everyone, and it was determined something had to be done. No one could believe it, and the rumor mill churned. Victory was near. The day they removed him was an unprecedented win for the underclasses! They removed him to the sixth floor where he swapped jobs with another manager who became our new boss. The monkeys swapped backs again and the offending manager went on day-trading and 'managing'...only on another floor.

I spent most of my time in the evenings complaining about the Hedgehog. It got so bad that one Saturday evening over drinks on the patio at WA Frost's restaurant, my wife, Laurie, had had enough. "Why don't you quit?" she said.

What an idea. If I quit I'd be happier, but somehow I imagined it to be dull not having the Hedgehog to complain about anymore. Could I find another job as good as this one? This job was safe and it paid pretty well. Renovating the kitchen would be impossible without a job, and I was having difficulty imagining finding any other job. But, I had had this job only about two years and I think I was still close enough to the Ryder truck crossing out of Illinois and into Wisconsin with no job prospects to remember freedom. So, I convinced myself I could leave and be ok with no prospects and no idea what to do next. I had watched another employee of the Hedgehog's quit a few months back after just a half year with TotalCom. He was beside himself with how things worked at TotalCom, or why people put up with it. My wife made me promise not to talk about work and to quit on Monday. I am sure she was just sick of hearing me gripe.

Amazing things sometimes happen. Strange coincidences that turn enemies into instant friends and realign agendas. Politics can make strange bedfellows. I walked into the office early on Monday. I waited for the Hedgehog to arrive and then I stormed into her office closing the door behind me. She smiled almost sweetly at me. No matter! That wouldn't work on me now. I told her, "I quit."

"Are you sure you want to quit?" She asked.

What? What was this? Some kind of trick?

What I didn't know was Ricky (her boss) announced the Friday before that he was leaving and a new branch manager would be starting in two weeks. She didn't know the guy, and over a drink with Ricky, she had been warned that the new boss would surely be looking at their attrition rates with the teams, not just the results. This meant that having people quit on her might not bode well.

Then and there it hit me. That screaming voice on my voice mail the first day on the job was another one of the Hedgehog's employees who had quit. It was Cathy! I had taken her place and here I was quitting. I am not sure why I never put it together, but that person was a broken soul who had once reported to the Hedgehog. I now understood Cathy's anger and frustration and her need to leave, but her desire to keep in touch. I meditated on the fact that even though she had left, she still checked in regularly. Would that happen to me?

No matter, I was resolved to quit. But the Hedgehog begged me to reconsider. It was surreal. She said she would talk to Lorna and try to get me on her team. She also asked if I would be interested in a data/Internet job in another sales segment. She heard that the Global Market group was looking for a new person to work on a big win we just had with a large regional bank. The Global group for anyone in our Mid-Markets team was a land of milk and honey. The rumor was they had smaller quotas and their job hinged more on managing existing relationships with people who already liked TotalCom. Compared to cold calling, this would be a dream come true. The Hedgehog poured on all her charm and I agreed to interview for the new job. I drove home. It was 10:30 AM and my wife was at work. I sat on the back steps to our house and buried my head in my hands. Was there really no escape?

I interviewed with the Global team the next week. They needed help with the installation of a new nationwide system for a bank. What I lacked in practical experience, I more than made up for in enthusiasm. I was sent to training for a week in Atlanta and came back ready to roll. I worked very hard and quickly found a place on the team. Commission checks were rolling in, but this role was more of an order taker than a sales job. No matter. The right place at the right time. Things were good!

Once the implementation was over, I had made a reputation for myself and was roped into taking on two other accounts. One was ordering new services from TotalCom, much like the bank. The other was a medical device company considering using us for their global business in Europe. This was new territory for me.

Things are always changing even when there isn't a huge revolutionary change in the wind. Europe was on the cusp of offering a single currency to bind together as a single economy that outsized the US and hopefully could outpace it with newfangled coins and bills. Businesses from around the globe were noticing the efficiencies and salivating over the new market. Medical devices such as pacemakers were a sure bet because baby boomers were hitting heart attack age. This became clear enough to me when a guy in our office had one over lunch. He eventually came back, but quit when he was offered a package a year or so later. The medical device customer had just purchased a distribution arm in Brussels with sales offices around Europe in the major cities. They needed to integrate systems with their inventory and health regulation systems.

I first met Steven by telephone talking over the opportunities. Steven grew up in The Netherlands and was hired by a joint venture partner of TotalCom's to sell TotalCom and our partner's services to the continent. Customers were clamoring for greater system integration, and a partnership was much less expensive and quicker to arrange than building from scratch. Additionally, European regulation had not lowered the bar sufficiently to allow a foreign company like TotalCom to build and compete easily on its own. This was all about to change.

The account director and I spoke with Steven almost every morning for months, strategizing on what we needed to do to convince US and European decision makers to purchase our solution for the next three years. This was a big bet, and we were spending a lot of time on it. Eventually, Steven came to the US to pitch the idea to a joint meeting of the US and European customer. I remember that the meeting opened chaotically like many US meetings do. Steven raised his voice and asked that we all listen to the business and technical needs of his European customer first before proceeding. A demure French-Belgian named Philippe nudged up his glasses and spoke for ten minutes on what he wanted to see. We used his ideas as a blueprint to work through the open problems and the deal was all but signed by the time Steven went home. I spent a lot of time with Steven when he came over and showed him around Minnesota. He would not forget this favor.

Chapter 6

A Brief Detour

My wife, Laurie, and I had planned a trip abroad. Both of us had been to Europe during our college years, but we decided to visit a pen pal of mine in Milan and then connect with other friends in Rome. The trip was fantastic and included a long layover in Amsterdam where we visited the Van Gogh museum. But as we were flying over Europe I started thinking about the cities where my medical device customer had offices. I felt like I knew them by heart. Paris, Berlin, Cologne, Madrid... I started wondering about the treasures they had. Certainly, many of these places were on par with Rome? The long flight home got me wondering how I would ever have the time to come back and visit all the places I so fervently wanted to see. I looked at my wife on our final approach to Minneapolis. What if I found a job at TotalCom in Europe? She smiled. We both looked out at the bleak, snow covered fields as the 747 touched down at the Minneapolis/St Paul airport.

The very next day I called Steven in Brussels. I wanted to know how to get a job outside the US. In his very Dutch style, he was quite positive about my inquiry and recommended I call a friend of his who worked at the joint venture headquarters office in suburban Amsterdam.

THE 30 YEAR PAYCHECK

I have heard many executives talk about 'their good fortune' and describe themselves as 'lucky' when asked about getting to their level inside a big company. Hearing this is cold comfort for anyone hoping to accomplish something specific in their career. The typical chain of events is "I was working in marketing and did a good job and then the boss asked me if I would take on managing a customer service department in Albuquerque. I did that and was asked two years later to lead a sales department." Each move starts out like a lateral move and turns into a bump up. The lesson learned is, do a good job and hope you get the phone call. I have to believe there is more to it, but I will never know for sure. These executives all seem to know they want to move up the chain and be in charge. This is why they move between divisions. It really doesn't matter where they work since they are predisposed to lead and execute. Whether it is a group of salespeople, customer service reps or a manufacturing floor, they can make it go and their drive enables them to keep climbing. For the first time in my career there was something I actually wanted. I wanted to work in Europe so I could see all the tiny cities I flew over on the way back from Rome. It may seem like a crazy goal, the kind of goal only a twenty-something would have, but nonetheless it was mine. I didn't care about the compensation package or the work they needed me to do. I just wanted to do it 'over there'. But when you have a goal and you are living freely to pursue it, magic follows.

My magical story unfolded like this: After bouncing from person to person in headquarters, I was finally introduced to Smith. He was a hardened TotalCom'er and really had no interest in Europe at all. He had moved his family to Europe in grand style, shipping his two big American cars and renting a 3,500 square foot house (enormous by European standards). Smith's role was to manage the channel sales to the largest customers in which TotalCom had implicit interest because they all spent big money with TotalCom back in the United States. Smith was a vice president and had a team of mostly American Expats working for him. But times were changing. Regulation around high tech companies was diminishing and the partners of the joint venture were licking their chops around entering each other's markets. They didn't need Total-Com, and the relationships were beginning to get tense. Expats who had been in Europe for a couple years were now being asked to leave or take local contracts. From Smith's angle, this was a nightmare. He didn't want more Dutch people reporting to him. I called him the day after he had delivered an ultimatum to 'go native or go home' to his group of expats. It also didn't hurt that he knew my uncle. Smith was intrigued from the get go and told me he would be in New York in a few weeks and wondered if I could fly out to meet with him.

I had never been to our corporate headquarters in New York, but with the help of an address and a cab I found my way from the Newark airport to the lobby of TotalCom Business Services. I didn't realize it until I was sitting there, but I had left my resume back in Minneapolis. This was going to be a long afternoon. Smith was a middle aged man, tall, balding, slim and wearing a golf shirt. He picked me out of a crowd by the front desk. He insisted on grabbing an early dinner with me and the conversation turned toward basketball. Smith had played hoops at Johns Hopkins under Jimmy Valvano. I was at Duke during Valvano's glory days at NC State. It was an instant connection. Smith told me I would need to take a local contract, but that he wanted someone like me to back fill a guy named Gene who was heading home from an expat stint. Smith wanted me to run a customer user group association for the big companies. It sounded like fun. Smith explained that the group got together four times a year, reviewed our performance and product mix, and made recommendations. After that, we were given the opportunity to wine and dine them at five-star hotels and restaurants. The money in high tech firms at this time was reminiscent of any big technology boom. It could not be spent fast enough. When the price structure started to falter in the late 1990's, it is no wonder the cash flew out the door and bankrupted so many of these companies.

Over dinner, Smith turned to tales of living in Europe. He hated it. Based on my one six hour layover, I was not a huge fan of The Netherlands either, but I couldn't wait to visit so many other places.

After dinner, Smith asked me where I was staying. I hadn't a clue. Smith panicked. "You are never going to find a hotel at this hour." He dialed furiously on his mobile phone. We drove around to the closer properties to find out first hand if they had rooms. On the fourth try, we found a vacancy. Smith stopped the car and looked at me.

"I'll hire you, but I need you there ASAP. Can you move before the end of September?"

I couldn't believe what I was hearing. I was being offered the job I wanted. The one I chose, for once.

Laurie was initially more shocked than pleased at the prospect of moving. We had a lot to do and needed to do it quickly. It was a lot of work renting the house, boxing up only what we could use in The Netherlands, finding a reasonably priced apartment in Amsterdam and getting our dog vaccinated. However, we worked at a dizzying pace to make the move happen. Smith had backed off on the date he wanted me to start. We were all set to spend Thanksgiving with my parents, drop off our car with my in-laws and head to Holland for a December first start date. On Thanksgiving Day, Smith caught up with me at my parent's house. "When are you getting over here?" I told him we flew out the next week. "Change of plan. I need you to come to Athens with us, can you fly out tomorrow?"

And so it would go with Smith, ever the schemer, never the organizer.

This was a great time in my life. My wife and I were trying unsuccessfully to have children and going to Europe for a year or so was a great diversion. I had been over there twice getting the apartment picked out and meeting the team. Everyone was cordial and I found a nice apartment off the canals near the Anne Frank house. I met Gene (the guy I was replacing). His office was a mess. Just by looking at it, I had a feeling he wasn't going anywhere anytime soon. It didn't matter that much to me, though. From the beginning, I was determined to see Europe and would worry about my job later.

Smith, Gene and I sat in the lobby of the Athens Hilton. Smith insisted on staying in the Hilton whenever possible and was a connoisseur of the 'Hilton Burger' on four continents. During the cocktail hour, we talked about the plenary session before us and how we were going to handle a few ornery customers. We had our plan and I excused myself to take a short nap before dinner to stave off jet lag. When I returned an hour and a half later, Gene and Smith were having a heated conversation. Back in Amsterdam, Smith told me that Gene didn't have a new job lined up yet and I would be reporting to him until he found one. Meanwhile, I would shadow him to learn the ropes.

Because I had a local contract, I didn't have benefits to return to the US twice a year like Gene had, but I had something better-- seven weeks of vacation (like any other self-respecting European professional). Immediately, Laurie and I started planning our free time. She couldn't work so she spent the week getting things in order and planning elaborate weekend train trips around The Netherlands, Belgium, Germany and even France. We checked off the greatest cities, museums and historical sites at a startling clip. Six months later Gene was still having closed door discussions with Smith and his desk looked about the same. One day in late May, Smith announced he was leaving. He had found another job with a US company and was moving to Los Angeles. Good for him. The only problem is that no one was left to remember Gene's promise to go back to the US. No one seemed to care either. I became a glorified secretary to Gene. I immersed myself in obligatory Dutch lessons to combat Gene's insistence on staying. I was peeved by Gene's decision and it felt like he was cheating me out of my own experience of running the Channel team and the customer group. Once Gene started asking me to arrange his travel, I'd had enough. I had become good friends with the local Dutchies who appreciated my interest in their language. I spoke much better Dutch in six months than Gene did after two and a half years. July and August are slow months in Europe. I spent much of the summer talking with a guy named Erwin who ran the partner relations team. He had openings and wanted to hire me. Things immediately got interesting when, in early September, TotalCom announced a strategic partnership with a British firm and an exit to joint venture relationship in Holland. There was a near-instant shake up in management and Gene came in over the weekend and cleared out his desk. He had a new job in New Jersey and was heading home at once. The user group remained operational, but a couple of guys from the Dutch side of the joint venture were hired to run it. I was moved to Erwin's team and the world was turned upside down.

I was worried that if I stayed much longer I would not be able to ever get back to Minneapolis. I was on a local contract which made it possible for us to stay as long as I had a job. I called the Minneapolis office to see how things were going. It was layoff season once more and this year the powers that be had elected to offer a retirement package to older employees. The Minneapolis Global team had been decimated. I was the youngest guy there by fifteen years when I worked there and now they desperately needed to hire, starting early the next year. I told them to hold me a spot. Truthfully, my wife was getting bored in Amsterdam and was ready to go. We had traveled frantically for over a year and what our life boasted in glamour, it lacked in stability. The Greek philosopher Heraclitus said you can never step into the same river twice because it is always changing. This river had definitely changed and become more turbulent. To top off our time in Europe, we arranged a month long tour of France and Italy by car to span my last days at the TotalCom joint venture and our eventual trip home.

THE 30 YEAR PAYCHECK

We flew into Atlanta on a one-way ticket. Our car was in storage at my in-laws house in the mountains of North Carolina. More than just the jet lag, everything looked odd to me in a familiar way. Try to imagine waking from a yearlong dream to find yourself back in reality. And reality was about to get even more familiar. It furiously snowed as we drove north to our house in Minnesota. Our renter had moved out and our furniture was still in transit. The house was empty, yet familiar.

I felt so clever. We had run the gambit and won. We left, had a tremendous experience, and returned. On my way to the office on Monday, the billboards were all new. Minnesota can be dreary in winter so suicide prevention billboards make a lot of sense. The one I was staring at above the tail lights in the pre-dawn, winter dark showed a large photo of a woman who looked a lot like my mom. "Feeling sad? Get help." it read, or something like that. I stared at that face. I can still see it now. I felt like she did. While I was living my dream job in Europe, my dreams stopped coming. When it was finally time to go, I just packed my dreams into a photo album and came home. I didn't have a destination other than back to my old life.

I was assigned some large global accounts: a manufacturer, an airline and global grain commodities company. The work was challenging, but I wasn't feeling inspired. I had chosen to go back and now I felt undervalued. Another colleague of mine in The Netherlands, Kent, moved back too. He got a job as a sales manager in Nashville, one full paygrade ahead of the job I took. The sad part? Kent was in charge of the corporate car plan for employees in The Netherlands and was a contract employee until the six months before he left. How could he parlay that job into a new sweet gig in Tennessee? I will end where I started. He got the job because he knew where he was going. For me, it was just the same old slog and a daily view of the suicide prevention billboard. Stuck in traffic, I sat listening to U2 singing: "It's a beautiful day, don't let it get away!"

Chapter 7

Another Detour and Falling Buildings

In 1998, deregulation was spreading like wildfire in Europe. Total-Com decided to leave a federation model that aimed at providing global service to multinational businesses with local flair. Multinationals were growing also. As domestic markets began to clog, multi-national businesses were forced on looking outside of their homeland for growth. Getting business from the rest of the world with the same business model, using technologies and new emerging logistics services, was solid gold for CEO's. Going it alone was a good bet if you could pull it off, because federations are frequently inefficient. The biggest problem is balancing self-interest versus federation-interest. This has played out again and again over time. About 250 years ago, our federation of colonies won independence. State's rights have been decreasing ever since. When we look in the history books, federations don't make it into the top ten. Rome and Athens come to mind. Both of these empires began as federations, but succeeded only when they converted to a central command model.

My belief is that apart from regulatory problems, European nations still lived with a fear of large centrally controlled states. Almost two generations and a world war later, the potential problems with these types of states looms large in the collective mind of the European (along with mistrust of other nationalities). This is certainly not a history book, but it is important to explain why many in government and business were moving slowly in Europe to build global solutions. However, the businesses which needed these global systems at reasonable prices kept pushing for it. TotalCom moved into a strategic partnership with a British company, acknowledging that it would be too expensive for either to build out globally in a way that would satisfy the multinational's voracious need for services. The chaos that was created as TotalCom and the British firm tried to convert customers to this new alliance could not have come at a worse time. New technologies and carriers were popping up everywhere as the dotcom craze hit its zenith. Irrational pricing and huge IPO's ruled the day. I watched as colleagues jumped ship to work at these new companies. Eddy worked at TotalCom for only five years (a very short tenure back then). He felt he was not getting paid sufficiently and walked out in a huff. When we saw him around town, he seemed to be loving it at a new global technology company backed by a French firm. He quickly started winning business away from TotalCom. His salary was higher and he got to play air hockey and pull beers from the company refrigerator at the end of the day. What revenue these smaller firms were generating was often at the expense of larger companies like TotalCom.

Meanwhile, for my new position at TotalCom, I moved into an office space across the street from one of my customers. The office was closer to my home and the commute was a lot shorter. We had a 3,000 square foot open room in a dingy three story gray-concrete office. When I moved in, there were four of us sharing the space. Eventually, we downsized but even then the office seemed too big and sort of lonely. It was almost creepy when you were there alone. I was working all the global accounts due to my experience in Amsterdam with our joint venture. TotalCom had left the relationship the prior year. I went on appointment after appointment trying to convince our customers to sign up for new services with our new British partner. In truth, we had nowhere to go but down. Some customers converted to the new service when it was expedient and properly priced. But whenever the competition was a penny less, customers invariably moved away from TotalCom. Some customers grew weary of change and figured it was a good time to bid all their global needs by Request for Proposal. We started losing out there also. My job was to keep customers happy while they walked away, and I actually helped them move their money away from us. I tried to bid aggressive prices. But once the sentiment had changed away from TotalCom and toward our competition, my bids were just formalities to keep our competitors from getting too over confident. One such competitor at the time was the French firm where Eddy worked. They were eating our lunch in Minneapolis.

I didn't know what to do. I wasn't earning much commission, and I wondered why no one would give me a job that I felt took into consideration all my wonderful international experience. I was treated like any other sales rep and, based on the rapid decline of our international revenues, it looked like I would not be working at TotalCom much longer. With all the dotcom mania, I wanted to share in the spoils. It was frustrating, but it was a two way street. What did I want? What was I looking for? Where could I use my international experience to help turn the tide? I didn't know. I had ideas of where I could assist, but my passion wasn't there. I half-heartedly looked for posted jobs inside the new TotalCom partnership overseas. I tried to bring back the old magic and luster by considering working abroad again. But I didn't have the will. I felt I'd be shot down anyway. Nothing made sense. After working in Europe, I believed that loosely combined and federated companies were better than big money partnerships. I felt that a diversity of opinions could always out-maneuver a big bank account of a single mega-company. One of my biggest beefs was the homogenization of services. I believed that a global business needed services that fit the culture of the places in which it did business. I set out to prove this. I took my Dutch skills to the Netherlands Antilles and back to Holland to convince local decision makers of my large customers not to leave and to move some services to the new platform by customizing them to fit the local technical desires. But I was just one person. Despite my heroics, many customers winced and went in the other direction, making the entire global infrastructure look the same. But one end of that equation was always unhappy with the decision.

As Winston Churchill was fond of saying, 'I kept buggering on.' I was doing a stellar job managing all the terminations of our services at one of my accounts. They were moving most of their business to a new foreign carrier called OneGlobe. This carrier was backed by French and US money. One day the purchasing manager at that account asked me if I would jump ship and become his new rep for OneGlobe. He said he had fired the last rep and he was demanding someone local in Minnesota to run the account. Having a sales rep in Chicago would not cut it for his global company. I flew to Chicago in late November. The hiring manager, Steve, reminded me of so many of the salespeople back at Communicate. He was looking for the one-call close and appeared to have just rolled in off a used car lot. Steve pressed hard for me to give my notice to TotalCom by December 1st. I learned later that he had a bonus check riding on getting the job filled. I am sure he would have hired anyone who didn't have two heads. What's the difference? He could bring me in, give me a two month honeymoon and then manage me out of the business and hire again...collecting yet another bonus if he could do it promptly. The salary was 30% higher than what I was making at TotalCom and the commission was bigger too-- with no cap. I came home to my pregnant wife and laid out the situation. Neither of us could think of a reason not to make the move.

My frustration with TotalCom was at a peak and I felt I could hurt them by leaving to join a competitor. During my exit interview I laid it all out. TotalCom was unsure what it was doing outside the US, and competitors were killing us. I ranted to my boss about how messed up the company was and that I was glad to be stepping away. In short, it was less than a gracious exit.

I started immediately at OneGlobe and even was able to collect a few deals before the end of the year. I was heralded as a great addition and started feeling like my old self. I began to network closely with the sales people who interfaced with Minnesota clients overseas, and we worked together to provide prices and services that made OneGlobe the perfect choice. Some of my newly acquired friends in Switzerland, Brazil and Egypt are still part of my LinkedIn network today.

My daughter was born in January and I was off to Paris the next week. Getting to know the people at headquarters in Europe helped me even more. I told Steve that I needed office space in Minnesota to get away from the crying baby. He relented. I found a shared office space adjacent to a gym, and I signed up to join both on the same day. I also asked for Dutch lessons to keep my language skills fresh. Again, Steve relented. Why had I waited so long to join a smaller firm? I had negotiated for more vacation and I was rarely too busy not to make my dates at the health club.

In June, we got the announcement. Eddy's company was merging with OneGlobe. We had a kickoff in Vaux de Viscontes outside Paris. On the bus ride in, we passed a line of prostitutes standing by an AGIP gas station on the side of the road. I was jet lagged, but something troubled me deeply. I had a bad feeling as we filed into an 18th Century chateau.

The meeting went fine, but the dinner in a hall fit for Louis XIV swirled with rumor. We obviously would see changes in the organization. Everyone wondered what the new company would be called. "Would you like some more red wine?" "Oui." "And more white?" "Oui, oui."

In July, the name of the new company was announced. Drum roll please! It was renamed the purchasing firm's name. I can still hear Eddy laughing over the phone. The logo changed, but there wasn't one shade of OneGlobe green in it. The writing on the wall was getting clearer. Back home, I asked the front desk to change the lobby directory to reflect the new name. I included the subheading "Upper Midwest Global Headquarters" for a laugh.

Another Detour and Falling Buildings

Steve was not amused. He had come up to visit me in the past, but mostly I flew down to Chicago every other week to join his team meetings and discuss business. Steve also was worried about the changes. He complained that my sales funnel wasn't big enough and started to lean on me for stronger monthly results. To top things off, he was mad about the hotel I had recommended. There weren't a lot of hotels near the Upper Midwest Global Headquarters, but the office space wasn't chosen for its proximity to hotels. It was chosen because it was convenient to my house and the gym.

"The perception is you are not looking hard enough for new business." Steve was in a poisonous mood. I explained that the perception was irrelevant. I was busting my hump. I also explained it was hard to win over a new market of mid-sized businesses when I was running global relationships and turning in the numbers on those customers.

It didn't matter. "Perception is reality", he scolded. But since I was a Philosophy major, I wasn't taking any of that Kantian stuff.

"No it isn't. There is reality, and there is what we think. I am telling you what is!" I said. I won the day by debate club rules, but I was about to lose the war.

I met with Eddy for lunch. Eddy was the only salesperson from the company that bought OneGlobe in Minnesota. I was the only ex-OneGlobe employee. Eddy laughed heartily about the new company. I walked away thinking, 'I have more experience, I am younger and better looking than Eddy. They wouldn't choose him over me? How could they?'

THE 30 YEAR PAYCHECK

The announcements started at the beginning of August. Eddy's boss was named the new CEO. Later that week: Old OneGlobe vice president of sales was made redundant. New vice president: Eddy's vice president. And so it went down the line until they got to the front line. The requisite week of stack-ranking and pondering took place. All was quiet. Too quiet. Our regional director (Steve's boss) had been decided upon. Jose was from Eddy's company and lived in San Francisco. He used large words incorrectly and fancied himself a globe-trekking swashbuckler. Jose organized a joint call with both sales teams. I should have flown to Chicago, but didn't. I spoke up on the call, and Jose was cordial. I called him afterwards and he didn't pick up.

The first week of September 2001. Beautiful skies from Minneapolis to Manhattan, cool and crisp. My phone rang. It was Steve: "I just got chopped. But USACo is going to take me back. Good luck." Steve had become an employee of OneGlobe because he worked for USACo which was an initial minority investor in OneGlobe. That afternoon, I got an email telling me to come to Chicago for 'an important meeting' on Thursday. My heart sank. I was getting the axe. We had a vacation planned starting September 14th for a week at the NJ shore with friends from Duke. But mostly, I was feeling mad. How could they do this? I wasn't done enjoying this lifestyle. Things change and you need to be ready. But I felt like I had left my family exposed. My daughter was an infant and my wife had told her employer she wasn't coming back from maternity leave. I had never been let go before. I always made it through the layoff because I was 'me'! I was the super talented guy.

Another Detour and Falling Buildings

Of course the best people are always retained, right? They get to stay for more layoffs and changes which they will always rise above, like pieces of flotsam from the Titanic. By remaining drifting at sea we survive. It is always better than being sent under the waves to Davy Jones locker in a layoff. But under water, the chance remains that we can break away from the current and reach another shore. Survival by bobbing over the waves only leads to more of the same.

I didn't see this coming. I was angry. I booked my ticket. Depart 6 am MSP-ORD. Re-turn 5:14 pm ORD-MSP. I was really angry.

Armed with Hemingway:

I rise before the dawn and creep out of the house trying not to disturb the baby or my wife who has no doubt been up late with her. I had slept like a rock. Before the cab arrives, I go to the bookshelf to grab something to read on the plane. I can't see a thing, and, instead of turning on a light, I just pull something off the top shelf. I grab my wallet and look at my computer bag. I figure I won't be needing my computer today. The headlights of the taxi spin through the living room picture window and I instinctively head to the door. This is going to be a long day.

"Boom! Boom!" We are under attack, the mist is burning off and General Franco's troops have a perfect view of our hideout high up in the hills overlooking Segovia, Spain. A mortar shell lands nearby and my heart goes cold. I can taste the sod it kicks up. I look for the commander. He is laying propped up under a craggily chestnut tree. He's laughing. As he does so bits of cheese and bread from his breakfast jiggle in his beard. Now he puts a wineskin to his lips. Some of it dribbles out of the corner of this mouth making his whiskers one darker shade of black. "Boom!" We are all going to die...and for what?

"Ladies and gentlemen we'll be landing shortly in Chicago. Thank you for flying United."

I am jerked away from Ernest Hemingway's 'For Whom the Bell Tolls' and brought back to the task at hand. This should be easy. No baggage to collect. Shoot, I don't even have any carry-on save this paperback book. I look out the window on my old hometown. It is a glorious day much like the ones we will see for the next week in St. Paul. I can see the traffic mounting on the Kennedy Expressway. We are coming in using my favorite approach over the lake. Sometimes I can even spot the old Communicate office when we come this way. But not today. Today I see the downtown. The Sears tower stands like a single lead soldier on the western edge of the loop. The OneGlobe offices are directly across the street.

I make my way to the trains for downtown. How could I have been so stupid? Of course they were going to keep Eddy and get rid of me. There is nothing to be upset about. They know him and I am an unknown. Enough said. The real questions is what have I been doing to prepare for this mess. What have I done with the extra 30% salary and the commission checks? The answer wasn't pretty. We had undertaken some home renovations we really didn't need and saved very little of the extra money.

The train lurches forward and they call out the stops: Harlem, Irving Park, Addison. I think we have enough to get by for a little while. Instead of 'dual income no kids' we are about to become 'no income, one kid.'

Like a lamb to the slaughter I walk into the office. I am the latest casualty in this private war. Inside Jose's office stand a pile of addressed manila envelopes. The top one has my name on it. Jose notices the book in my hand and asked me what I am reading. I show him. "I was an English major too, kid", he chuckles. Nervously, he pulls the contents out of the envelope and reads the pre-approved legal statement to me. My job is being eliminated and they are happy to write me a recommendation. The meeting is over as quickly as it began. How could I possibly know that we are three business days away from the September 11th tragedy? All eyes are upon me as I walk out of the office and make my way across the cube farm to the door. I smile as best I can and head back to the train.

A few hours later at the McDonalds in O'Hare, Hemingway's Robert Jordan is hiding, wounded behind a bush. He clutches his rifle and takes aim at an enemy patrol making their way toward him. He is determined to take a few of them with him before he is cut to ribbons.

I decide that I must move on too. No matter what is next. The flight is delayed and unemployed I arrive home in the dark. Robert Jordan has been dead for hours, but I am still standing. I silently climb the stairs and enter my daughter's bedroom. She is asleep in her crib under a cotton blanket with small rocking horses printed on it. I look at her and watch her breathe. In. And then out. Defenseless.

I drop into bed exhausted knowing, however, that tomorrow the sun also rises.

Chapter 8

Searching

Ibegin immediately with the search for a new job. I have not kept my
network fresh and up to date and it is an uphill battle. I start working
like a fiend. I call everyone I know to get the word out that I am available and I start combing the job boards. I have a three month severance,
but I feel like those ninety days are eating me up inside. I am terrified
that I might not find work, but my sense of entitlement makes me determined that our family takes our vacation. I can look for a job as easily
at the New Jersey shore as I can at home.

I am driving to the office to get cracking on some job leads when I hear
the news about the attacks in New York, Pennsylvania and Washington.
I try to pretend that it isn't such a big deal, but no one is answering
the phone. I go down to the lobby of the shared office space of One-
Globe's Upper Midwest World Headquarters. People are aghast. I am
too wrapped up in my own problems to fully understand or feel the
tragedy. Watching the screen, I very selfishly think: 'Please God, not
today...'

Our family's flight to New Jersey is cancelled and we drive instead.
On the Ohio turnpike there is a feeling of camaraderie and resolve
against the apocalypse. Flags fly, people are courteous, the bathrooms

are spotless. I stay on the phone the entire time. I need work. Fast. My family doesn't have the cash reserves and, although unemployment would suffice for a while, I feel that if I do not find a job quickly, the process may become very protracted. I answer job ads for insurance sales and franchise opportunities. Even the bottom feeders are spooked by 9/11. Almost every conversation ends in a continuance (instead of an offer), and a promise to keep in touch.

After a week at the beach, it is time to go home. 'To what?' is the only question. I convince Laurie we should keep driving. We visit my brother-in-law in Washington, DC and then drive to Duke University. Standing on the quad in the rain as the students shuffle by, I have a strange memory. I remember the person I was when I left this place. Now I can hear him. He is screaming out to me in the rain. Our baby is crying and I can't make out what he is saying. I turn my back on the quad, and we walk briskly to the car and drive away quickly.

At my in-law's in Asheville, North Carolina, I work the phones and even sheepishly call TotalCom to inquire about openings, but it is apparent enough that we are on the run with an infant in the back seat who is often screaming. When I suggest we drive to Florida, Laurie puts her foot down. It is time to go home and face the music.

I feel like I have lost my identity along with my employment. The people at the job-center, where I need to register and work each day in order to get Minnesota unemployment checks, reassure me that my feelings are normal.

But why? At what point do we turn an imaginary corner and begin getting our identity from the logo we wear or the work we do on behalf of others, and not from our own skills? The only way I could seem to shake that work identity was to stay on the road.

I started having a recurring dream that continues today whenever the stress level is mounting at work. I am walking into the refurbished offices of Communicate in Chicago. It is my first day back and they have a cube all set up for me along with a cold calling list. Some faces are the same, but others are new. Everyone seems to be having luck on the phone setting appointments except me. The truth is my heart isn't in it. I know I need to hustle to make the rent, but I just can't seem to make myself care. I feel like a loser, not because I am not having any luck selling, but because I cannot seem to make myself care.

During my unemployment I kept myself busy. When I wasn't job hunting, I did push-ups. The gym membership was a thing of the past. I also started painting the house. I kept thinking, it would help down the road if we needed to sell. These are the stupid things you think about when you have been fired.

Something was changing in me. I went through a week of feeling utterly depressed. I interviewed in half empty offices of small fry technology companies that were wondering if they would make payroll on Friday, or if their venture capital money would hold out. I looked around and tried to picture myself working at these places. I couldn't. We were coming down to crunch time. I needed to find something.

I was torn away from painting the front porch on a chilly fall morning by a phone call. It was TotalCom. They had an opening and wanted to interview me for a job in small markets. Before that could happen,

THE 30 YEAR PAYCHECK

I needed to take the data test. The human resources person trained in with me about the same time that I started. I reminded her that we had trained in together and that I had sold data services for many years. I had only left TotalCom eleven months ago. No matter, she was sticking to the rules. Oh yeah, I also needed to come downtown and show her my passport or social security card to prove citizenship. Wait a minute? Why did I have to prove citizenship? I had worked there this time a year ago! I couldn't believe it, but I held my tongue and arrived the next day with my documents. I waited three days to get an interview. Each morning, I called my contact explaining that I had not heard from anyone. I remembered this song and dance from my initial hiring and I didn't have time to wait three weeks for a result. In truth, I couldn't believe that TotalCom was still hiring. It became clear later that the events of September 11th hadn't caught up to the behemoth yet. TotalCom instituted a hiring freeze a few weeks after I was eventually rehired. In the meantime, I interviewed with the hiring manager and her boss. I knew them both, but they were cold as cucumbers to me. Both of them knew I could sell and brought a lot of knowledge and skill, but they wanted to make me pay for deserting them. They told me I would have a sales module where I would hunt for new business and would need to do a lot of cold calling. They both assumed I didn't know anything about that, having been in the Global group during their recent memory. I smiled. I can cold call, I told them. This was a challenge with a chance for a path to redemption. This was my kind of fight.

Chapter 9

Minneapolis Act II

The offer letter came two days later. I took the bus to the office. It was a warm day for late October. I stood at the doors of the Minneapolis TotalCom building on Fourth and Madison Avenue. I swallowed hard. It felt like a large slab of crow was inching its way down to my gullet. I walked in the door and forced a smile. I stayed smiling and rode the elevators up. No one was in the Human Resources manager's office so I tried to look surprised as my new/old colleagues walked in and headed to their cubes. Eventually, Ms. Human Resources showed up. She wasn't expecting me until tomorrow. No matter. As long as I was cool with not getting paid for that day.

She pulled a laptop out of drawer behind her desk and handed it to me. It looked familiar. I opened it. It was my old laptop! I was given a cube in the worst conceivable place in the office. Much younger hires had found their way to a window facing cube. I sat on the high traffic internal aisle adjacent to a small conference room where people liked to congregate and gossip. I plugged in my laptop and found my old login worked. That was pretty cool. The icons on the Windows desktop stood right where I had left them. It was like being an archeologist of my own past. I clicked on the email icon. To my surprise it opened. Then the most astounding thing happened. A year's worth of email from people who did not know I had left, and a mammoth supply of spam filtered into my inbox. I had more than 1,000 emails to look at. I responded to people who wished me luck in my new position from the previous November by telling them I was back working at TotalCom. How convenient was that! My third time back at TotalCom started much differently than the previous two. I was given a "low share" account list by my new boss, Diane, on almost the first day. I knew Diane, from my first tour at TotalCom. She was a small business sales person and always found a way to make good money. She was always at the top of the charts. When her old boss got promoted, he promoted her instantly. She really wasn't sure she wanted to be in management, but did not refuse when asked to lead. My reputation as the guy who made it to Global markets then worked overseas and came back was known to her and she was hesitantly confident that I could succeed.

After the initial re-entry shock, I set to work-- a new man at Total-Com. I wasn't going to let any opportunity to shine go by. I cornered the market by being ruthless in my sales techniques and exuberant in my offer to help others. I studied the compensation plan for myself and my superiors in order to satisfy us both. I pulled every lever with my customers to hit both my metrics and the metrics of my superiors. Truth be told, I was working with a bunch of dog accounts that did not buy much from TotalCom. I compensated by taking a line from Tom's (the favorite son under the Hedgehog) book, by convincing the customers to change services regularly. These changes counted toward my monthly quota at the time. Few others in the company had figured out how to work the system like I did. My ship began to rapidly rise as did that of my boss. I was the tide that lifted all boats.

Minneapolis Act II

Times were getting tougher and tougher for TotalCom. It had lost the global partnership with the British firm when TotalCom's CEO left and a new CEO stepped in. It was rumored that the new guy was put in place to control spending and make us attractive for a buyer. We were running out of money. The sales team was told not to give any more price concessions in exchange for new contracts. This is basically the game that Tom had mastered to his great benefit eight years earlier. I knew it didn't make sense, and now we were being told the same thing formally. I thought about the big 30, 40 and 50 thousand dollar checks that Tom got each January. They would be no more and therefor I needed a new strategy also.

I came back to TotalCom on a mission. The mission was me. I was going to make it through this down-economy. I was going to do that by looking out for me and my reputation only. No more pie in the sky ideals and no more Mr. Nice guy. A large company that manufactured for TotalCom was having difficulty with its TotalCom account manager. I was called into Diane's office to discuss it. She laid out the situation. The TotalCom rep named Jackie had told the customer's Chief Information Officer that she would not lower prices on existing business with TotalCom unless they covered the decrease in revenue with new business purchases.

The situation was complex. This company was a huge supplier to TotalCom and our slow-down was affecting their ability to pay for our services. Diane asked me what I would do. I told her I had read that we were going to spend some money on building out our international business based on the British company's departure and that it must mean we are evaluating vendors. I thought that this balance of trade could be discussed in an effort to smooth things over. Diane nodded. The next day she met with the customer. When she came back to the office, she asked me if I could take on the account. She had convinced the Chief Information Officer to renew for the global business and to give us half of their US business by reminding him of the new purchase TotalCom was about to make. In return for the help with strategy, Diane moved me onto the account. Diane proposed that Jackie get half the commission for the sale and I get the other half. "That's fine," I said, "but Jackie needs to help me with the project management of the new service implementation. It is only fair."

I was playing my cards. I knew that Diane could never allow Jackie to help with the project management, considering that the customer no longer wanted to speak to Jackie. Diane took the bait. She saw my point, but also acknowledged it would not work to have Jackie help. I suggested that 75% of the commission go to me and Jackie get 25%. Diane concurred.

Next, I met with the client and convinced them to change the proposed design. Each change in the design meant that I didn't need to share the commission with Jackie. Technically, each change amounted to new business sold after her departure. I maximized my payout at the expense of Jackie. My monthly numbers skyrocketed but I built a list of enemies on my own team. My interest in winning and staying on top seemed to imply that I wouldn't have many friends. However, having a lot of friends was never a reason to rank a sales person higher during layoff season. Being nice seemed to be good way to get let go. Understandably, Jackie was now a nemesis.

Diane's self-interest propelled my fame and good name up the command chain. A reorganization brought the advent of a new role called the Client Business Executive. The new role meant an instant increase in pay. The adjoining layoff culled out sales people who were not cut out for the new role and their positions were largely back-filled with more junior sales people. Basically, the new role was a way to lower the overall payroll while keeping a few, key, longer term employees in charge of the biggest client relationships. I was one of the first people asked to apply for the job and take the application testing. The test measured how business savvy one was. It was the antithesis of the data test I had taken for Lorna seven years ago and again a few months before to get my job back. I studied by doing Google searches on business trends and passed with flying colors. Nobody congratulated me on the sales floor, but I got many kudos from the people with office doors. With Diane's assistance, I sat down to hand pick a new sales module of accounts.

The housing market was exploding, so Diane gave me a window manufacturer as a client. A local insurance company was in merger and acquisition mode and always good for upgrades, so I got that one, too. Diane asked if there was anything else I would like to add.

In the years since I had worked in Holland, the medical device company that initially acquainted me with Steven, my Dutch friend, had continued to grow. With the dissolution of the TotalCom joint venture and the subsequent bumpy years with the British, they had left Total-

Com and moved to another provider. The account had some TotalCom gear, but mostly they were working with others in the US and abroad. I had watched them closely when I returned because their revenue had shrunk so much with TotalCom that they were now in the middle market module. Jackie was working on the account and they were up for renewal. Diane saw the fire in my eyes. I wanted to win that account and I felt I had all the needed skills to do so. She thought about the situation with Jackie. We had a small laugh about the equipment company. Diane thought that there wasn't much potential with the medical device company. "Are you sure you want this?" She asked. "Are you sure you know what you are doing?"

On this one I did. My blood was boiling. I wanted that account. Diane relented and Jackie reluctantly took me out to introduce me to the new team. All the people I had worked with in 1996 were gone and a new cast including a new Chief Information Officer was on board. I set to work replicating the success from before with the new team. I got the name of the new customer contact in Belgium and requested support from our new and improved TotalCom international team in Brussels. The global team in Brussels rejected my first request saying that the opportunity was not big enough. I pushed back and finally got connected with Vincent. He was the low man on the totem pole in Brussels and was made my partner on this opportunity based on the confidence level the European management team had in my deal.

It was around this time that I first became acquainted with Mickey. Mickey was new to the Minneapolis office, but not new to the mix apparently. He came from the British partnership and after the break-up, was orphaned in a land far from the home office. TotalCom took him on to lead our new solo global venture. A new service had been cobbled together with some assets from The BigData Company that TotalCom had purchased. Mickey got trained and was reluctantly ready to help. He didn't like TotalCom or our team. He had done a stint with TotalCom under Lorna way back and was run out of town on a rail like so many of her hires during the Tran days. But Mickey knew enough to be pleasant and dutifully came into the office. I introduced him to my global customer. The director, Jim, was fairly new to his role and was disappointed by the fact that his European subsidiary was using a different services than the one in the states. This made his life a headache and diminished his power in the organization. His counterpart in Brussels, Sven, had an equal place at the table with him in front of their Chief Information Officer. Jim liked the brand new network that Mickey proposed to him. It was a perfect match for Jim's technical needs. But Jim worried that the 'made in America' band would be problematic for Sven. We offered to help, but he wanted to handle it. He was planning to travel to Brussels soon and make the pitch. Mickey and I bonded over the positive feedback and began having lunch together in the break room each day. I pulled out my PB&J and Mickey bought a soggy sandwich in the Skyway.

Mickey and I became inextricably tied. To this day when I pull up LinkedIn I see his face. "People who viewed your profile also viewed". To tell the truth, this is a legacy I am not especially proud of. It is a reminder of a different time in my life. A time when I held a very different attitude. Others in the office were as wary of him as they were of me.

THE 30 YEAR PAYCHECK

They knew him from his last time around at TotalCom as volatile, and he kept to himself during his first months in the office. The feeling was mutual. I was the only person engaging him for help with my customers. He was happy to work with anyone as long as he would be allowed to run the show. His excellent presentation skills and intimate knowledge of the global network made him a hit with my customers and I was happy to give him control if it meant we would win new business. Over time, I realized that he always had an answer even if he wasn't sure. Often wrong, never in doubt. His confidence was a breath of fresh air over other TotalCom'ers who constantly 'needed to get back to you' on loose ends. I saw how this affected people and did not call him on it. It accelerated our conversations and everything was moving along at record speed. He left the heavy lifting to me for pricing, forms and internal approvals. But the local, folksy charm he used with the Minnesotans didn't endear him much with global clients. This is where I came in. My time working in Europe was invaluable at forging relationships outside the United States. Additionally, from years of processing termination paperwork for my old Global accounts, I knew the systems and processes inside out. I also understood the importance of the global customers and I worked the phones with Vincent to make sure he was delivering the right message. I kept close tabs on how our Brussels' customer was feeling about the deal.

Jim's meeting with Sven in Brussels was a disaster. They couldn't see eye-to-eye on anything. I heard about it from Vincent who had talked to Sven immediately afterwards while Jim was high over the Atlantic licking his wounds. Vincent said that Jim played the power card with

Sven and Sven put up a wall saying that he would make the decisions in Europe and if he had his way he would pick someone other than Total-Com just to keep autonomy.

When I talked to Jim the next day he downplayed the discord, but said that Sven was leaning toward another provider. He was going to talk to that provider too, just to give them a fair shake for the US business. It was crazy, though. Sven's European provider had no expertise in the US. Jim also wanted to talk through a robust integration between the two eventual vendors in the likely event that we needed to link the two systems together.

Mickey set to work with a list of why it made sense to use one and I socialized the list with Vincent. I told Vincent he needed to push hard. In return for using us globally, we offered Sven his own billing in Euros, as well as a service manager and operations center based in Europe so that he could keep his power base. Sven started to melt. He wanted to meet the US team and he flew to the US. Over breakfast he put on a good show, acting like he still was not convinced. He said he didn't want to be duped into buying a US product from a US company. We needed to show him our commitment to meet him halfway. We offered to have his engineers, Jim's team and the global sales team all meet at our European operations center in the UK. He said if we could convince everyone in the same room to move forward with this solution, he would support it. All I needed was a ticket to the UK.

This was not going to be easy. Money was scarce. It was so scarce that the ranks of the company were becoming paper thin.

THE 30 YEAR PAYCHECK

One of my colleagues likened the situation to the old TV show Star Trek. Scottie, the engineer, was constantly asked by Captain Kirk for 'more power' or to have repairs completed faster. In his Scottish accent, Scottie would reply shaking his head, "I'm doing all I can captain, we just can't do that!" That was us. Back then, if you needed something done you just kept calling up the command chain until you got a sympathetic ear. Those years, I found myself talking to so many Executive Vice Presidents (and even an officer or two), making urgent requests from the bridge for more power. By linking the requests to new sales and more revenue, especially with our brand new global product, I was able to get the attention needed to give my customers what was needed. The interesting thing was that once TotalCom was on better financial footing, calling up the chain was outlawed by company policy. To the relief of so many I badgered with urgent requests, the upper management was now untouchable and it was safe for them to sit in meetings all day without the danger of being interrupted by a need from the field. Being able to effectively communicate, make requests and give concessions was a newly acquired skill for me and the secret to my success at that time. My requests were air tight and this elevated them over much bigger customers with a bigger upside and consequence to TotalCom. That was of no concern to me, though. I saw myself as an island. I knew the reality was another downsizing in the fall and I didn't plan to be on that list. Zero sum game. I didn't need to outrun the lion, just the other sales people. Popularity and, heaven forbid, collaboration, were not in my vocabulary. I figured that when others lost, that was a good thing for me. I didn't have to necessarily win all the time, I just needed to stay ahead of my peers.

Diane had moved back to a sales role on her own volition and we both started reporting to a director named Frank. Frank is a lot like me, spontaneous and outspoken. So, when I approached him about going to England to tour our Operations Center with my customer, he laughed and asked why? Was I trying to get him to pay for my vacation? Then I told him that Mickey needed to come too. Once he finished laughing, I showed him a detailed estimate of the cost of the trip and another estimate of the value of the new business. He quizzed me as to why the international team could not handle this on their own. I responded that this meeting was about everyone seeing eye-to-eye and understanding what the other needed politically out of the deal. A handshake was needed so that each could be reminded that the whole team needed to win. This cut across both of our companies and the geographic teams. Frank asked me what would happen if we didn't go. I looked him in the eye and told him we might get the US business, but we certainly wouldn't get the international business. Then I told him it was possible we could even lose the US business. The argument was sound and it rang true. I have to hand it to Frank. He stuck his neck way out with our vice president and up the command chain. International travel needed to be approved from the top. It was eventually approved for just me to go. I knew I could not sell this without Mickey. He could be a liability in the office, but he was pure gold with the customers. I continued to push and finally, they relented, Mickey and I were off to England!

The visit was filled with charm and honesty and we hammered out a deal. Each afternoon Frank called me asking if they had signed yet. I could see the sweat on his brow through the phone.

We returned home with a clear intent to move forward. But then something funny happened. The US customer started getting directives from his Chief Information Officer asking him to include a few more non-standard options into our deal. Frank told me I should start looking for a new job if this did not close. Our President of Sales, Curtis, happened to be flying through town and I suggested he come out and meet the Chief Information Officer. Curtis is a huge hulking guy with false teeth and fingers too big for a Blackberry, but he is probably the nicest guy you will ever meet. He believed in the sales team and unlike so many of his predecessors, seemed more concerned with us and our needs than with the mid-level managers. Curtis arrived at the customer location with Loni, the vice president, demurely at his side. He nearly broke my hand shaking it and asked what he could do to help. I explained that he just needed to listen and then we could see if the requests could be addressed. Loni looked uncomfortable. This was a risky situation for her. What if it didn't go well? What if the customer did not buy? What if I was a total imbecile and had misunderstood the client's intentions? On the other hand, Curtis looked relaxed. He smiled. He liked situations like this—where work was actually getting done. After all, he was running a global sales team on a shoestring budget, trying to keep our books competitive in the event of a corporate raider. What did he really have to lose? He most certainly would be removed if we were bought. He appeared to genuinely love the sales hunt.

Minneapolis Act II

When the Chief Information Officer walked over to greet us, Loni looked paler than I have ever seen her. We sat down and rolled up our sleeves. Curtis took a number of action items and pinned others on Loni who nervously adjusted her glasses each time she was asked to do something more. Then came a bomb shell. The Chief Information Officer asked that Mickey be removed from the account. I asked, "Why?" When I was on vacation, Mickey had lost his cool with Jim, and I had not heard about it until this meeting. He had lashed out at Jim and Jim wasn't going to have any of it. We walked out of the meeting with a new and clear path forward.

We won the deal and Mickey was pulled off as support. Truthfully, I really didn't need him anymore. I was past the sales phase now and onto project management and implementation. Many of the other action items from the meeting were squarely stacked on Loni's desk. Loni was even on the hook for monthly meetings. I chuckled inside. It was fun to see Curtis kick Loni around like an old sock, and Loni looked like a schoolgirl valiantly following up and running after the details. Meanwhile, the accolades started rolling in. Frank was relieved and asked me to go 'sell another one'. That is what I like about Frank. You knew where you stood with him as a friend, but business is just business. For Frank, you get up in the morning, drive to work, sell things and then go home. He taught me to control the things I could control and let everything else pass. I became a believer, slowly. I still tilted at windmills, but I began to see the wisdom of conserving emotional and political energy. Not too long after the sale, there was another reorganization and Frank was promoted to a vice president role in small markets. My new boss was Leslie. She was my boss's boss when I had walked out to work for OneGlobe. This wasn't going to be easy. Luckily, I was walking into her office with a huge sale and a stacked deck of other accounts under my arm. I had the largest monthly quota by far, but I didn't complain about it. I was still blowing it away. Leslie was a lot more reserved than Frank and our styles were different, but she kept an open mind, so I decided to do the same. We worked well together and her method of suggesting instead of telling what I needed to do to improve my career enabled me to slowly change for the better. Some things were off the table. She wanted me to become more of a mentor for my peer group. I saw this as a self-centered attempt on her part to make more selling machines like me out of the others. I didn't see anything in it for me at the time and continued my all-out assault as an army of one. If we were going to lay off the entire sales force before we got bought, I would be the guy turning out the lights.

I often fantasized about that moment. Everyone had been let go, except me. I win. How crazy is that? September 11th and my layoff had made me into this monster. Leslie shook her head and smiled because she was making money as my manager and with such impressive numbers her job was as safe as houses regardless of my methods.

My international customer grew by leaps and bounds. I partnered with other global TotalComer's in South America and Asia and we were kicking it. My window manufacturer was also growing with the housing bubble of the early 2000's and I could hardly keep up with the orders. Money was rolling in and no one could touch me. Regardless, the overall environment at TotalCom continued to be a challenge and in an autumn down-size, Leslie departed and moved to Atlanta. They did not replace her and Diane and I started reporting directly to the Sales Center Executive Director, Donny. Diane had also hand-picked a great set of accounts and she was the only person remotely close to my results. We enjoyed a healthy competition that sometimes leaned toward the toxic. Mickey was sore about being pushed off the medical device account, but got over it and stayed close to me in order to stay in the limelight. Our success together had also given the rest of the sales team a reason to warm up to him. That same year, I was sent to Royalty Club. Royalty Club is the big sales award where the top sales people get a trip to Mexico with their spouse for three nights of wining and dining with top TotalCom executives. The trip took us to the Ritz on the Mexican Riviera. Our fearless leader Curtis spared no expense on this trip despite TotalCom's money problems. He saw these events as a major motivator for top performers. He was right. I loved it. I once heard Loni downplay the sales incentive trip's value to the company when I became a sales manager years later. She felt that it was luck-of-the-draw to go anyway. She said that sooner or later everyone would have a customer who would propel him to the big trip. I didn't see my big win as luck. I think she was thinking of a different day and age at TotalCom. Times had changed since the days of being a monopoly. The world was a rougher place. I am not sure Loni ever saw it. She was a vice president in Minneapolis for the entire seventeen years I would spend there. Every year must have blended into another for her. Up and down went the charts. This year's big win was a future big loss. People came and went. From her vantage point, keeping your head down, making the safe bets and obsequiously grinning at anyone above your pay-grade was the secret for success. Walking on the beach in Mexico, I told Laurie that I felt really good. It wasn't because I had been chosen for this trip, but rather because I knew why I had been chosen and I knew what to do to be chosen again. Sure enough, I was back at Royalty Club two years later. But shortly thereafter, the specter of Loni's up and down theory came and smacked me right in the chops.

Each year got tougher. Customers changed personnel and I had to re-negotiate contracts. New customers wanted different things. They wanted things the services were never designed to do. They hated the status quo and I represented it. Desperation started to settle in. The new director, Carl, at my international medical device client told me it was my job to make him look good. I looked at him and knew my work was cut out for me. Making him look good entailed curtailing his spend with TotalCom. Meanwhile, TotalCom was paying me to do the opposite. We had a conflict. He had no interest in letting his company's budget grow with us no matter what. Over the past five years, we had quickly become one of Carl's largest vendors. I asked to give someone else a chance to run the account, but the request was denied. Donny was having none of that. I needed a new approach. I was looking at my first down-year in the last five and the walls seemed to be closing in. Diane was on top of the sales rankings and she wasn't letting me forget it.

One of the device manufacturer's divisions in Los Angeles started making trouble for Carl. Instead of working with the division to partner, Carl pushed TotalCom to deal with his own problems on the west coast. He blamed the problems on TotalCom products and positioned me as the guy to fix it for him. I agreed to make regular trips to LA to meet with the division until it was sorted out and I started to make good friends with many of the staff in California. It was during one of these visits that I got the news that TotalCom was being acquired. The long march through the desert was over for TotalCom. It was over for me too. I honestly thought that this was very good news. We had money again. We had a future and significantly, we were keeping our name. I remembered from the OneGlobe merger that it didn't matter who was buying whom, but the new name meant a lot and did foretell who was going to be laid off. Management was decided by the company name... at least that's how it had worked out before.

It was a picture perfect day in Los Angeles. Out of my hotel window, the mountains looked so close I could touch them. I had a ritual I followed in Los Angeles. I stayed near the airport and in the morning drove out the 5 Expressway to San Fernando. I would always make a stop at the San Fernando mission to collect my thoughts. I am not Catholic or overly religious, but inside the Mission it was easy to slip away from the craziness and see California as it must have appeared to the early Spanish settlers: The quiet of the gardens, the splashing of water in pools, a staff member carrying a metal bucket as he silently prepared to water some hanging plants. It all brought a sense of eternity and peace to me. The drip, drip, drip and rapid evaporation of the drops from the bottom of planters, reminded me that everything ran its cycle from creation to destruction. On this gorgeous morning, I began thinking about my future. In this moment, surrounded by such beauty, it hardly seemed to matter. Back in Minnesota, I would have frozen to death in the time I walked around this courtyard. It all felt as if I was getting pulled into something sinful. I made my way back to the red rental car. My next stop was always the restaurant just across from my customer's regional headquarters. I ate food there once, but never again based on a bad result that followed. Instead, I got a cup of coffee and waited for the hour of my appointment. My feet stuck to the floor and I fiddled with my smartphone looking at email after email.

My main contact in California and new friend was Martina. She was not particularly high up in the company, but she had her finger on the pulse and was a good friend of the divisional vice president. We talked about our kids and she once gave me great ideas on where to camp near Big Sur for our family vacation. We talked on the phone almost every day and I was there for her when she had a problem or request. She was very transparent to me. Never mind our burgeoning relationship, just the fact that I flew 2,000 miles every thirty days to talk to her was enough reason for her to give me the inside scoop. The internal politics she faced in the office were not much different than mine, and up to now there was little in it for me. I dutifully listened to her complaints.

Today, things were different. Her vice president, Pool, came into our windowless conference room. He didn't sit down. He said he was having a problem with Carl back in Minnesota. I agreed that Carl could be difficult to work with. At that moment, I began a deal with the devil. I didn't know how dangerous it was at the time, but I was soon going to find out. Pool had heard the news about the acquisition and shared that his division had done a lot of work in the past with my company's new owner. Then he related that Carl was trying to put an end to that relationship by working directly with hardware vendors and making decisions on behalf of all the divisions. Carl wanted to be a clearinghouse for all projects yet his team was so small and underfunded it would undoubtedly cause delays and headaches for Pool. The new Chief Information Officer in Minnesota supported Carl's efforts for central control and was making Pool foot the bill. Pool felt ripped off in every conceivable way. We spent the next few hours talking about how the new, combined TotalCom could help him. I wasn't even sure what hardware I was selling since the merger had just been announced, but Pool assured me it was everything he needed. Pool shared that they were building a state of the art manufacturing plant in Venezuela and he wanted TotalCom to bid on doing the entire project from design to implementation. This project alone would be as big if not bigger than the original sale I made. He also shared that they were building another plant of similar size in Malaysia after this job was completed.

I agreed to help. I knew that this was poison to Carl, but it was just what I needed to keep my streak alive. I kept our little project in confidence with Pool and Martina. We were talking almost daily. I was spending less and less time with Carl, but that suited him just fine. It was all in a day's work in making him look good. Eventually, he caught wind of what I was doing. I told him that Pool and Martina had asked me not to mention it to him. This made him furious. I guess this wasn't in the spirit of assisting him. I felt bad, but my job was to sell things. Carl was determined to not let TotalCom win. But my quote and Total-Com's advantages as a global firm were impossible to beat. Any other solution involved smaller firms that didn't have the resources to send people to Venezuela. No matter, Carl wasn't going to lose this battle. But I had one more rabbit to pull out of my hat. I had the desires of the California division and a solid relationship. Carl had run roughshod over them and they felt bruised and wronged. The Chief Information Officer got a call from the Pool and they set up an internal meeting.

I sat on pins and needles that week. Martina sent me short bursts from her Blackberry during the meeting. Things sounded bad. It was later compared to a 'steel cage match' where wild animals, having been forced into tight confines, rip each other to shreds. The meeting went late. The next day an extremely somber Martina returned my call. I had been calling her the entire morning. She told me that TotalCom was getting the business for the new plant. All of it. Then she told me that she had quit. Somebody had to take the fall for the dysfunction this situation had created in the company and it landed on her doorstep. She said all the right things after that: "It was time for me to go, I had been thinking about a change, let's stay in touch." But it was all very hollow. I knew that this had come down to me. There was a way to do this differently. Winning wasn't as important as this. Nothing was as important as people.

Things only got worse. I invited Carl to lunch to patch things up. He ate without saying a word, methodically shoving food in his mouth like a steam shovel. It was one of the more uncomfortable things that has ever happened to me. In the car on the way back to his office, he laid it out. He felt I had destroyed his relationship with everyone in his company and created a rift that probably would not heal as long as the current people were still around. The last thing he said was, "There is only one thing I do to vendors who go behind my back like this, I fire them!" 'Good luck with that,' I thought. Our services were under tight maintenance contracts and we just signed our largest contract ever in Venezuela. I didn't realize he wasn't talking about my company. He was talking about me.

After the initial big sale, Donny made sure I got the best cube on the seventh floor. Under the new ownership, Donny became my mouth-piece to get things done too. He negotiated on my behalf with Loni and escalated my requests with the rest of the new regime.

A few months later, I sat looking out the window nervously squeez-ing a blue ball that had a corporate logo on the side of it. I was sure glad to be back in first place now, but something was changing. It felt like my luck had run its course. My phone rang. It was Donny. "I need to tell you something, kid. I just got whacked." Donny sounded shocked. He was nowhere as shocked as I was. He explained that there needed to be balance in the sales management ranks and he was collateral dam-age. Donny had played his cards right. He always took the safe route and had a stellar relationship with Loni. Loni had even hired him. But either Loni couldn't or didn't stop a 30 year vet from going down. For Donny, TotalCom was his family. He was now being asked to leave home and not come back for Christmas. I couldn't believe it. Donny had often talked about the monopoly days. Like Loni, he viewed them as the good old days. Once Donny had moved out of his office, I went in to see what was left. This was a ritual of mine. Whenever someone quit or was let go, I would always check their desk to see what they left behind. I would find pens and loose change this way. But I did it for other reasons too. I often would sit in the vacated chair when no one was around either early or late in the day. I thought about what it meant to be that person. I even collected the plastic printed name from their cube name tag holder. I kept them in a special place in my desk. The stack was getting thick. When I went into Donny's office, I found a treasure trove. I took a gold plated paper weight with the TotalCom logo and a date on it that might have been given to him as an award for beating his sales plan that year. It was hideous enough that he didn't take it when he left, yet important enough to let it sit on his desk all these years. Donny and I stayed in touch. One day he came into the office and came by my cube. I tried to position myself between him and his scrounged paper weight. I did a really bad job of it. He noticed. His jovial demeanor turned to one of pensiveness as we continued the conversation. He wasn't mad, but I could tell he was worried about me. He had let go. He had to. There was still time for me, but how much?

A while later, when I finally got in hot water with Loni, which you will hear about soon, I went to Donny for advice. He counseled me not to worry. You are safe, he told me. They will never get rid of a guy like you. This amounted to the biggest compliment you can receive at a big company. When I finally left Minneapolis, I put all the trinkets and name tags in a bag and threw them directly into the dumpster in the lower level of the building. I wanted to make sure that no one else at TotalCom could ever get their hands on them.

This was the guaranteed 30 year paycheck. I started wondering if 'never being gotten rid of' was enviable or not. The upside was steady income and health insurance for the family. I was a responsible provider to my children, whether they needed a flu shot, a molar drilled or if they wanted to go summer camp. Great. I know that a lot of Americans and many in the developing world would kill to have this stability and living standard. But just keeping my mind fixated on what others didn't have and I did, was not good enough. Is that really where I needed to place my mind for the next fifteen years? Since getting my job back at Total-Com, I swore never again to be caught off guard as I was at OneGlobe. I was determined to save in such a way that I would never let others hold control over me. For my peace of mind, I didn't want to be at the mercy of middle managers or anybody else!

The next day my new interim manager, Tim, called me. I knew the guy because I sat around the corner from his office. He came from another technology firm and was an affable gent. I figured I would be reporting to Donny's replacement once that was sorted out so my relationship with my interim was cordial. I was more or less a lone wolf in the office. I had won my top position back on the Venezuelan deal, and I spent my days trying to keep my top position and never letting anyone see any weakness in me. Tim and I hit it off immediately. He was complimentary about the job I had done and played to my ego.

He asked what I wanted to do next. Next? What did he mean? I thought about it. Donny's sudden departure, the squeeze ball, and my running-out-of-luck feeling all gave me a reason to pause. A year ago, I would have dismissed the question as a way of messing with me, knocking me out of pole position for commissions and, more importantly, my high likelihood of surviving a layoff. Tim coaxed me further.

"Have you ever thought about sales management as a viable next step?" Shoot, I had never had a true direct report up to this point in my career. Tim convinced me that even if I didn't want to be a team manager forever, it was a skill I needed if I wanted to move up in the company. I couldn't expect to be carrying a sales bag forever. Maybe he was right. Maybe this was a good time to consider my options. Best get going to my future destination before this house caved in.

Ever since I was laid off a new, recurring conversation was taking place in my living room after the kids were in bed. My wife and I were on a war path to reduce our expenses. Having been caught off guard by the OneGlobe layoff, this was the other side of the coin to my hard-hearted approach in the office. A Spartan home-life was created. At first, it was easy to reduce our expenses. We cut as many subscriptions as we could. This included pay TV and the gym. We bought some weights at Target and started running outdoors. This may seem like no biggie to those of you living in California or Florida, but dedicating oneself to year round outdoor running in Minnesota means perilous sub-zero runs over ice and snow. We cut back on heat, bundling up at night under blankets. We started making our own laundry detergent based on an article in the paper written by the Everyday Cheapskate. We also began shopping the sale items at the Rainbow discount store which was a distant cousin to the other better-heeled retailers in St Paul. We even found a program that gave away free meat and vegetables to anyone who wanted them regardless of economic position. I began taking two stage showers where I cut off the hot water during lathering to save on hot water.

Minneapolis Act II

Every bit of incremental money we saved was compartmentalized and placed into tax deferred retirement accounts and invested in funds that carried the lowest maintenance fees. Each salary increase I received was instantly saved by increasing the deduction I took for my 401K. Commissions were stockpiled into emergency funds. Someone at work once asked me what I do with all the commissions. When I told him I pulled weeds on the weekends, drove a fifteen year old car and shared a beat-up lawn mower with my neighbor, he was incredulous. He couldn't understand it. Where was I putting all the money? I remember how it felt to be unprepared for a layoff and I never, ever wanted to be in that position again. As it turns out, we eventually needed all that money and then some to break away from the same old broken record at TotalCom. But for the moment I was like Mr. Scrooge in my counting house huddled behind my gold pieces and fending away anyone and anything that tried to get near me. Living like this seemed to best fit my work lifestyle too. Being conservative was good. Our soft spoken Lutheran minister grew up on a farm in Northern Minnesota and told many tales of thrift and endurance of hardship in the country. I felt like I was fitting in to that culture of mending what was broken and saving to provide during hard times.

Tim called me into his office one snowy Friday in late February a few weeks after our career conversation. He looked white as a sheet. He had just gotten off the phone with Loni. The Chief Information Officer of my beloved international medical device customer had called. They wanted me off the account. Even then I felt I had more power than I did. "Well, just tell them 'no'!" I said. But that isn't how it works. The largest sale I had ever made, the one that won me a spot at Royalty Club for the second time in three years, had also gotten me removed from the account. Things were starting to unravel. My other customers were hitting tough economic times and stopped buying. Making my monthly sales quota was getting more difficult. A veritable flu was settling in on the economy that surrounded my accounts. Tim gave me a pep talk and showed me my new account list, based on the reshuffle instigated by my big account firing me. It was a group of deadbeat castaways that my peers offered to 'help' me with in this time of need. You definitely reap what you sow and 'what comes around goes around', but that is all cold comfort when it is happening. I certainly didn't feel like going out and changing my ways at that point. In fact, if anything I was determined to be more ruthless than ever. Otherwise, how would I ever get my house back in order? I didn't want to be on that layoff list.

That night under the stars on a frozen skating pond, I whirled around in a wide circle. I could feel a warmer breeze. Spring would be here soon. And summer was never far behind. Summer meant fall and fall meant layoff season. Hopefully, the new owners wouldn't need to keep reducing the force. So far that had not been the case. As I packed my skates and herded the kids back to my rusted blue Subaru and took off over the frozen roads of St Paul, I mourned the loss of my big account. I wondered what I could have done better both for them and my company. Did I really need to choose between safety and me? Did I make the right choice choosing me? How was I going to keep doing this for another fifteen years? It felt like a death sentence.

Minneapolis Act II

The sales executive who assisted me with my accounts was named Bea. She was younger than I was with a bubbly personality and positive outlook. Her dad was a dear old friend of Loni's and because of her relationship with Loni she was disliked by many on the sales floor. We got along because we both had few other friends in the office. Bea had ridden the ups and downs with me over the past year or so, and now we had to start over. I felt alone. Bea scheduled three hours for us to meet one Monday and talk about the new accounts. We dug through files and looked at analytics and webpages trying to figure out how to bring the magic back. Although I tried to remain optimistic, I just wanted to cry and give up. My pride had taken a deep bruise. I kept up appearances with Bea and we began working our plan. At first, everything we tried seemed to fail. Decent opportunities that existed in the files crumbled to dust. We missed our number the first month with the new accounts and there was little hope for month number two.

My old boss Frank gave me a ring one day in late winter. Since we had last spoken he had worked as a sales vice president in the small business group at TotalCom. He had come into his own with the new job and was having a blast traveling from coast to coast and kicking down his objectives with a fun team. I tried to hide my disinterest in his success. "Great." I said. I know how to empathize, but then I just didn't have it in me. Frank sensed this and cut to the quick. He had a problem sales center in Minnesota and needed to remove a low performing sales manager. He wanted me to apply for the job. He pointed out that we worked well together and I "really knew what I was doing and knew how to succeed around here." I was flattered. It was the first good thing that had happened to me in a while.

From the very beginning I felt like the job was mine, but in reality others applied for it too. One of them was my old colleague Mickey. Frank knew Mickey, but he was not a fan. Mickey was a vocal opponent of Frank's when he was our sales director, and even private conversations have their way of coming back to people. Of course, Mickey thought the job was his, and held a grudge against Frank for years afterwards when he was not chosen. I had no experience managing people and this job had a huge people management component. Frank is still a friend of mine and he's a real class act. He recused himself from making the final decision. Instead he had a broad team from all across the country do group interviews and rank each candidate. I prepped for the interviews by coming up with ways of showing that I had managerial skills. I grasped at straws. I kind of managed Bea, for example. I talked about how I helped her meet her goals and discussed career aspirations with her. Similarly, I kind of directed Vincent's work in Belgium. My interviewers were hating the first forty minutes of my hour interview. I tried to speak a language of which I was not even sure of the pronunciation rules. Later, one of the interviewers said that the instant messenger chat at that point in the interview was trashing me up and down. But then I got the challenge questions. They started peppering me with questions on how (specifically) I was going to get the team to make their numbers my first month on the job. This awoke my ego. I started rattling off systems, tools, methods and customer scenarios I would mine with each sales person. I painted a picture that I would do the whole thing single-handedly if I needed to. I wasn't going to be part of a team that was in trouble. That wasn't an option. There was an eerie silence. I wasn't sure if they liked what I said and frankly I didn't care.

I got the job. In my mind, my stunning innate managerial skills (based on zero experience) won the day. It is much clearer to me now that my passion clinched it.

My gift of passion was decidedly not something prized by a big company. Passionate cogs or wheels do not make the machine lumber faster. They can create beautiful local movement, but in the end they are discarded for more reliable and slower replacements. Safety favors mediocrity. Risking a venture to the true north might mean hitting an iceberg. The amazing thing was, this interview panel was turned 180 degrees by the sheer force of my will. It was a singular win. Perhaps they figured that a dynamic leader like Frank could keep me reigned in and make it work.

The last person I needed to talk to before I was given the official offer letter was Ethan, the Senior Vice President. Ethan didn't want to know about me as much as he wanted to put me on immediate notice. I was taking on a team that was in last place in the country in monthly sales results. Ethan said that it was up to me to make changes to turn this around. "If you tell me that everything was ok with the team," he explained, "I will assume any performance problem is attributable to you. Furthermore, if you are not performing, it is my job to address that." I understood where he was coming from and I was ready.

Frank called me at about 6 pm the next day as I was walking over the Mississippi river from my bus stop to my house. The job was official. I got a twelve percent raise.

I had beaten the odds, but this team was in shambles. They disliked my predecessor and were wary of the lone wolf from the seventh floor with a reputation that preceded me. In the small markets, sales teams each had a partner sales person who sat in a call center in Denver. I had a counterpart who managed that team and instead of my eight team members to learn and get to know, I also had to learn their inside counterparts and the relationships between each.

At first I felt completely overwhelmed. I looked at the pages and pages of account names I was given by Thom, the outgoing sales manager. He spent several hours going through the accounts. He had maps of down state Minnesota and Iowa on the walls. He showed me where the major centers of customers were in the outlands. He also kindly gave me possible itineraries to visit these customers including a loop out to Omaha where our lone man in Nebraska was based. When Tom finally left, I felt utterly depressed. Would I waste my days driving around the windswept interstates of the Upper Midwest only to fail and be yelled at each month by Frank? I decided to reserve judgment until I had a chance to talk to everybody. I sent out meeting requests that were promptly accepted except by one person: Sally. Sally and Thom were buddies and despite the fact that her numbers were no better than anyone else's, she was protected and thus sad to see Thom go. She had come out of the mid-market group I was in. During one of the reorganizations she found herself in small markets and I had not heard much about her since. I decided I would deal with Sally later.

The first person I met with was Annie. Bubbly, young and pretty she was thrilled to see me, and relieved that Thom was gone. Frank had handpicked Annie to be on the team and didn't ask Thom for his input on the hire.

This is a strange, yet common practice at TotalCom. At least one third of any book on managing people is devoted to making good hiring decisions. Hiring and firing is expensive business and moving people on and off of the roster is therefore taken very seriously. So seriously that a hiring decision at the first line manager level is rarely made by the manager. Frank is an easy-going guy, but when things were not going well in the sales center, the control freak in him came out. The upshot of having hiring decisions come from above is that no one feels accountable to the poor souls who are brought in. They are viewed as temporary and this attitude drifts into their psyche and right back to the company. Loni was the ultimate 'mover of pawns'. What often happens is the hiring executive makes a big bet on someone who he saw as 'perfect' for the job. Once in place the executive puts zero investment into coaching the person or even checking in to see how he is doing. After all, this activity is up to the supervisor—the person who took no part in making the hire. The supervisor, feeling resentful and disconnected from the new employee, lets them fail and make mistakes in front of others thus proving that they were the wrong person for the job. In Loni's case she would then blame the supervisor for the failure, even if the hire was all wrong. And the cycle continued.

The corollary to this dynamic is when a group of sales people rise up and trash a manager in one voice. As I have previously mentioned, this occasionally happened. I learned from Annie that this had also happened with Thom. He too, had been reassigned to another group and not removed from the organization. I immediately suspected Annie was the ring-leader. It didn't worry or bother me. One thing I learned over my past fifteen years in sales was you only get to throw one manager out. After the bad boss is removed and you are given a new one, you can't really complain anymore. Not liking one individual is one thing, but having a problem with his replacement as well makes you look like the problem. Based on the hiring process I just outlined, it is extremely likely that even if you push out a boss, the next one will often be about the same. Never underestimate the defensiveness of the second manager too. Being gun shy of an organized team can make life difficult for vocal members. I wasn't worried though. Thom and I could not have been more polar opposites and Annie warmed up to me at once. We talked about her accounts. She told me she had a great relationship with her inside sales partner partner in Denver and planned to exceed her quota for the rest of the quarter based on sales in her pipeline. I looked at her results for the past couple of months. She had reported $0 two of the last four. She explained that she was protesting Thom and turned in nothing in order to hurt him and have him removed. That was a gamble I had never seen before or since. It is amazing what emotions can make you do. Not turning in any sales has a direct effect on take home pay and can get you fired for non-performance. Thom had put Annie on a performance plan. When he told me about her, he didn't seem emotional at all. He explained that when the numbers for the team sank, Frank told him to put anyone on a plan who was not making his quota for the year. The picture started to come together for me. Thom was disconnected and ran the sales team like he would a gas station. He made sure it was staffed at all times and the restrooms were clean, but he didn't give anyone a reason to pump in the high test! He put people on a plan to follow protocol and not with any intent of either helping them succeed or ensuring they left the company. His lack of a plan had translated to Annie as a lack of concern for her. Once that dam is breached, there is a lot of force behind it.

But now Annie was ready to move forward. We went through her sales funnel and what she had teed up for this month. When I looked at her accounting for the sales she made, it looked too low. I told her she was cheating herself if the sales came in higher than expected based on upgrades that almost always happened during implementation. She told me that the team in Denver logged all the sales based on what she gave them and they used a set of standards their manager had given them to report the sales. I wrote in my notebook: 'All sales results will be reported from Minneapolis, not Denver.' To me it was crazy. The Minneapolis team was judged (and paid) on the results and yet they used another team to estimate a sales size and therefore worth. The Denver team was not paid on the sales. They were paid by making sure customers stayed under contract and gave us a good score on our annual customer service surveys. I gave Annie a rough idea of what I would estimate each of her sales at based on a formula I used in my last job. I showed her the difference in the reporting amount. Then I pulled out her compensation sheet and showed her how much more she would make with a more aggressive estimates that came to fruition nearly all the time. She was astounded. By the end of the hour she had increased her forecast and would bring in the quota for two members of the team this month.

Next up was Randy. He was new to TotalCom and had worked at a number of technology firms. We knew a lot of the same people from the interviewing frenzy during my 2001 job search. Each of the depressing jobs I had looked at and winced, Randy had actually done. Randy came to Minnesota from Des Moines to work for a start-up. The company failed and he quickly cycled through a pile of money he had amassed in an executive role years before. Randy was bitter about work life, but happy to be employed and not to be under Thom's thumb anymore. His numbers had suffered from lack of good estimating by his partner in Denver as well. Randy was confused by the amount of reporting and non-sales tasks we had at TotalCom. He had worked with smaller more nimble companies and couldn't wrap his head around the customer service aspects of this job. In his previous roles, those tasks were left to the service manager. Any sales person slowing down to help a customer with an outage or some other non-sales task ran the risk of not making quota, and therefore being asked to leave. As he spoke, it was apparent to me he too was having 'a disconnect' with his Denver partner based on his desire to always sell. I admired his enthusiasm and I understood the tenacity that had kept him whole at the other companies. But it was tripping him up at TotalCom. I could help him. I knew how to work the system with the right proportion of selling to customers and selling internally to people who held your reputation in the palm of their hand. Randy was open to learning my survival method at TotalCom and I felt I could help him stick around. I told him and everyone after him that the Minneapolis team would now take charge of reporting sales, and that I wanted to see every estimate that was being put in for accuracy. Randy was on board. The remainder of the team less the Omaha rep were too new to know anything. They were happy as clams to have a job at a company the size of TotalCom and they worked from home as much as possible. This core group was not impressed with Thom, but they couldn't have cared less. Annie had worked them up and they had added their signatures to the articles of war against Thom. But it was not their battle. Because of their lack of skills, these guys were hated by the Denver team. The Denver team was trained on the systems. These were the same systems I had learned by trial and error over the past twenty years. The guys in Denver liked to complain, but also liked the fact that they had job security because they knew how the systems worked. The clueless majority of my team would run me through the ringer over the next few months helping them get work done that the Denver guys said they were too busy to help with. I turned around requests faster than their Denver counterparts. When four people in Denver are being smoked by one sales manager in Minneapolis who also has a full time job as a peer to their boss, they quickly kicked into high gear. My next conversation was with my peer Mort, in Denver.

Mort is cordial and productive. He is testing me out on every level and trying to drag me into a protracted discussion about Thom and what went wrong. I listen and don't take the bait. We move to a discussion of the team relationships. I knew I had to give Mort a quick win and then hit him in the teeth with my demands. He characterizes most of the team relationships as broken. I agree and tell him what I would do to fix this. To no one's surprise, he wants more focus from my team on getting surveys returned and keeping customers happy. I say I think that is a good idea and promise to talk to my team about it. It is my turn: I tell him I want my team, not his, to report the sales from now on. Ready for a battle, I hold my breath. Mort is delighted with the idea. This is a huge time suck for his team. They also have to face audits and questions from the compensation team. I am sure Mort thinks I am dumb for asking for this but I am scoring points with him and his team.

Owning your destiny is critical. Frank urged me in the new job to work on things I could control and not worry about things I couldn't. During my building years in mid markets I did one better. I imagined all the outcomes that could come from any given situation, and thought of the ways that each outcome could benefit me. For example, if a customer bought a new service, I would be grateful for the new revenue. If they decided not to buy it, I would suggest needed upgrades to keep their existing service working smoothly. I quickly noticed that when I left my results in the hands of others, there would be delays and problems. The more I controlled, the better chance my winning streak would continue.

I spent the last week of the first month doing nothing but assisting my new team with entering results. They had never done it before, so I had my work cut out for me. In one way or another I entered all the results for my eight person team. It was the biggest month the team had had in over a year. My phone rang off the hook with accolades from everyone, including Frank and Ethan.

Our team meetings are every Monday at 8.30 sharp. After a quick celebratory pep talk I turn the focus to helping out the Denver guys. My team is not taking the customer surveys seriously because they are not paid on having them completed. I tell them to start scheduling lunches and asking for signatures. We set a goal to get all the surveys done in a month. This is an extremely aggressive goal, given the lack of interest by our Minneapolis team so far this year. But everyone is energized by the big month we just turned in. In between a busy month of appointments, I meet with each sales person and learn that we are about to have an even bigger month. Annie is turning up the steam. The positive environment is motivating her to succeed, and the rest of the team is trying to catch up.

This results in an eBay like effect. That month, on top of getting a record number of surveys completed, we crush our numbers. We are quickly rising from the bottom of the heap. I look at the top performer. It is Thatcher in Portland, Oregon. His numbers are high and consistent. I look at the forecasts and hatch a plan. It is October and we are going to give Thatcher a "trick or treat" surprise. We plan to beat him. From my conversation with Mort, I learn that Thatcher is an operator. He takes advantage of his west coast geography to see where everyone else is going to end the month and makes sure to do slightly better by using his time zone to his advantage. He has his team put in just enough in sales to beat everyone else late in the day when the rest of the sales teams around the nation have gone home, and squirrels any remaining sales for the next month in order to do it again. Knowing what the competition will do enables Thatcher to work the system. In talking with Annie and Randy, I calculate that we can beat him at his own game if we stay up late enough on Halloween. We just need to let him play his cards and keep our results low and then, when he finally goes out trick or treating, we beat him with a dose of his own medicine. This year Halloween falls on a Friday. While it is a bummer to spend Halloween and a Friday working the plan, it actually favors us because even Thatcher's Pacific Northwest team will want to get their candy-corn early. I have the whole team plugged in and waiting. 9 pm, 10 pm. We put in a sale that puts us dangerously close to Thatcher's number. Thatcher's team counters by reporting another sale, after all it is only 8 pm in Portland. Our premature move costs us but with any luck he is not on to our game. At 10.45 Central Time (only 14 minutes until the systems closes for the month) we dump in all our sales.

Thatcher never knew what hit him. On Monday, he calls me to congratulate me on a 'good' month. Frank is overtly amused. The team is quickly climbing the stack rankings.

It was amazing to me to see the change in my Minnesota team. Monday morning meetings became a time for camaraderie and banter. The team that was once ready to point to anyone but themselves as the reason for the problems was now working together to help each other succeed. But there is trouble in Denver. Our change in fortune doesn't help the Denver team at all. They are paid on different metrics and they have grown accustomed to blaming the Minnesota team for any deficiencies in their performance. The Minnesota team is now high-performing and making them look bad. Despite greater cooperation with the client surveys and good results, Denver is looking to trip up the team's momentum. As is so often the case, one team's success necessarily means another's failure. The zero sum gain that says 'no one wins without someone else losing' stands in the way of a total transformation.

I did everything I could to keep the momentum going. I had never felt so powerful. I had shared my passion and it became infectious. An entire team was now firing on all cylinders. This was one of my proudest moments. But I still had problems with Sally and my guy in Omaha. I booked a ticket for Omaha and asked Frank if I could put Sally on a performance plan. Sally had remained silent during the transformation we were having and I wasn't going to let her poison this well. Sally left the business and we continued to roll, but Denver was getting more vocal. They claimed the Minneapolis team was taking advantage of the reporting plan for new sales.

But something amazing happened. The client engagement kept improving and the depth of sales reported each month was so great that the voices in Denver were shouted down. I empowered my team to take control of new sales situations and leaned on Mort to get his Denver team to comply. The Denver team which had previously been running the relationships and not pushing for new sales, now sat in the back seat. With a team driven by success, not surprisingly the new sales flowed.

Nobody could believe it, least of all me. I was unsure whether I knew how to lead, and here I stumbled onto some powerful principles. Motivating a team means empowering them to lead in the things they do each day and own the results. If the front line employees are not given the chance to lead the charge, they will not feel empowered and will always point to other factors to explain lack of success. But if they are given the chance to call the shots (and own the results) the chance of success increases, along with job satisfaction. One reason this worked so well with my team was that they were all fairly new to TotalCom. If during my first years at TotalCom, I had been given the same latitude I gave to my team, things would have been much different for me. I felt like I was awakening.

Our Senior Vice President, Ethan, who had given me the stern warning when I first took the managerial job, decided to visit the sales center. He wanted to see what was happening. When the sales technicians and subject matter experts heard that Ethan was coming, they too decided to come to town and bring their management. About ten managers and specialists arrived in Minneapolis and it was our job to keep them busy seeing our customers. We built a large board and took over a conference room as our war room to coordinate. Each team member set up dozens of appointments and the whole thing went flawlessly. On the second day of our sales blitz, we all gathered for a late lunch. The plan was to go to a team building event after some brief remarks from Ethan. Ethan put down his slice of pizza and addressed the team soberly. "This has been a great event," he began, "but I am going to miss the rest of the festivities." He was being called back to TotalCom headquarters. A large reorganization was underway and he was needed. I said goodbye, he shook my hand and congratulated me on a great job. I was on top of the world.

Minneapolis Act II

The reorganization came down in the next few weeks. The small business group I was part of would be disbanded and rolled into the mid markets group where I had come from just a few months before. This meant redundant management would have to be collapsed and led to the possibility that my job would be eliminated. It also could mean Frank's job, possibly even Ethan's. This year's layoff was squarely targeted at eliminating middle management. I went into the Thanksgiving holiday not knowing what to expect. Rumors swirled wildly. On the Monday after Thanksgiving, everyone was informed of their status. "Are you safe?" became the watchwords. The week before the decision Frank called me at home. "I need to stack rank your team." This means ranking each person from first to last in case more cuts were needed in the sales teams. We went through the group and ranked them from one to eight. It wasn't hard to do. Frank then confided in me that I should expect 50% of them to be let go. I swallowed hard. He asked me to join him in his office as he read the verdicts to them on Monday. I did not know as I sat there which team member would go. The pawns in this twisted game are always controlled by bishops and rooks a few levels up. "Headcount" is just that. A number. On Monday, two guys named Ray and Rich down in Omaha lost their job to redundancy. I was spared the chopping block. Ironically, my interim boss Tim in the mid markets group had his job eliminated. Essentially, I took his spot. Replacing your old boss through an attrition process is nothing to be proud of, but under the circumstances, it was a relief. But I was still riding high from my turn-around story. Never mind that half of that team had just been let go. I would begin to manage my old team plus the people who used to be my peers under Tim. I have read about how difficult it is to manage a team of people who were previously your peers, however I figured after one hit I had this management skill down cold. The other piece of good news was that Frank had been retained. He would be vice president for the entire mid markets and small business group that had just been merged in Minnesota. The only thing that made me uneasy was that Ethan was no longer our Executive. Loni took that role for the Midwest. I thought about how many layoffs Loni had survived. Many more than I did. I am sure she was sitting very smugly in her office looking out at a frozen downtown Minneapolis no doubt. She looked out over her kingdom. The TotalFinancial digital clock on Fifth Street flashed 10:30 am/ 15 F.

A ritual of mine was that each time I survived a layoff, I would go out to lunch alone. I generally went to a nice sit down restaurant. Most people hate eating alone, but I actually enjoy it. At my private luncheons during these layoff years, I would calculate how much my 401K would grow in the next year, what vacations we would take and how I would wow my kids at Christmas by buying even more toys, candy and bric-a-brack. I also fantasized about the bottle of Christmas Scotch I would purchase for Laurie and me to consume. Snow swirled at the skyway windows as I made my way to lunch. Below, I could see my team assembled behind the window at Keys Restaurant, drinking Bloody Marys. The 'safe' and 'unsafe' of the new merged team. The afternoons after these layoffs were completely useless. The teams disengaged entirely. Everyone sat wondering who would get what accounts from those laid-off and Frank spent the afternoon in Loni's office figuring all that out.

The lone wolf ate his chow alone. I made success happen once and I could do it again. What about Loni? What did I care? She was Frank's problem and as long as Frank sat between me and Loni, everything would be fine. My phone vibrated with a new email. Surreptitiously glancing at it, I saw a meeting request from Loni for the new leadership team that will take place each Friday morning.

Everyone is gone and I am sitting in my office with the door open. Frank wanders in and we talk about nothing. He and I are about the only people on the seventh floor. Frank starts trying to convince me he is in good with Loni. "It should be fine", he says.

"I think Loni likes me," I muse. "She sent me to Royalty Club... twice."

"Why don't you go home", says Frank. "It is going to be a long week."

The largest of the mid-market accounts are assigned to my counterpart Nick's team. He came from the company that purchased TotalCom and is one of the few vestiges left in Minnesota.

I am given everything else. With ten direct reports, I have more people reporting to me than ever. But the survivors in my combined group are not real excited about working with each other.

New structures are needed when existing ones do not succeed. Combining sales segments is a logical cost saving move through combining middle management. But it often doesn't address the underlying reasons the expected results aren't materializing. And where are the expectations coming from anyway? Often, industry consultants are paid top dollar to benchmark where they think sales should be for large businesses like TotalCom. These benchmarks become quotas and an employee's success or failure are linked to them. It is logical enough, but this process throws out the critical thinking. If we are underperforming, why? Does it have to do with product pricing, support, reputation, marketing? Or is it a function of sales efficiency and effectiveness? If the sales teams are losing too many customers, how are we paying them to keep customers happy? Controlling the things we can control is the path of least resistance. So, if the management controls organizational structure, and if there is a gap in results, a change in organizational structure is often just around the corner. It is laughably simple and simpleminded. It avoids all the difficult questions that could fundamentally change the company for the better.

There is a large human toll to these reorganizations, especially at large companies. First, you will recall the fear factor that drives people to want a 30 year paycheck. These employees will take a lower salary and even poor treatment day in and day out in return for safety. Reorganizing can be terrifying and paralyzing for these employees. This is one reason an expected lull is often forecast after a reorganization. It is a bit like watching the smoke clear after a bomb hits. Employees driven by safety are unlikely to march into a cloud of dense smoke with the hope there is a reward on the other side. But once it has cleared, they are more than happy to work in a wasteland.

There is also a darker side. Regardless of whether the reorganization breaks up a group or adds new members, there is always a perception that some have benefited by the changes and others have been punished. Intent and blame is laid from the first line manager up to the CEO, who is scolded for her irresponsibility in requiring goals which could not be attained in the previous year. The pecking order is decided and the bullies are ready to squash those not prepared.

In retrospect, the pecking order on my new team set me up for failure from the outset. The account managers handling the larger accounts thought I favored my previous team and didn't understand or help them enough. Meanwhile, the remnants of my previous group felt under-valued because they did not have the bigger and more important accounts.

When any squabble occurs on earth, the surest thing that will stop it is the Alien Syndrome. The Alien Syndrome teaches that all strife on earth would end if our planet was suddenly attacked by aliens from outer space. For my team the alien invasion took the form of Nick's sales team in Minneapolis. He kept most of his sales team through the reorganization. They were seasoned vets, and cohesive. They planned to make an example out of us. I was already thinking ahead to the next fall and the next layoff that would surely come after this train-wreck re-organization. Most likely, we would go down to one sales manager and I wanted to be sure that would be me. With Frank at the helm, I thought my chances were good. But Frank is a fair individual. If Nick played his cards right, and had the results to back him, he could very well be the last man standing in Minneapolis. Luckily for me, Nick used his first impressions to take personal pot shots at me and my team, and to try to wrangle our few decent accounts away from us. Nick remembered my implosion on the medical device account and saw that as a weakness to exploit with Frank. Thankfully for me, Frank did not see it that way, and he had recent proof that I knew how to run a team effectively. Frank was a new entity for Nick, and Nick wasn't over the fact that his old vice president had been let go. Like the rest of his team, Nick was predisposed to disliking Frank. Allied with this opposing team was my old colleague, Mickey. Mickey also was still smarting from being passed over for my job, and had an axe to grind with me. He came by my office in early January and congratulated me on surviving and welcomed me back to mid markets. He cautioned me that being a manager in mid markets was going to be a lot different than in small markets. Whatever. I tried to keep it cordial, as he would be supporting some of my team's accounts. Mickey joined Nick in taking shots at Frank whenever possible. Mickey also built a boycott on engaging Frank with customers on Nick's roster. Things were really broken. The in-fighting was so epic that no one cared about winning. The sales people all believed that by sabotaging each other, their chance for survival increased. Total-Com had to employ somebody to look after accounts in this geography, and each felt he was doing TotalCom a favor by doing that job. Again, no need to outrun the lion, just the guy next to you. Needless to say, the magic disappeared and we struggled to make our monthly quotas. Somebody, I believe it was Mickey, even contacted corporate security claiming that individuals on my team were cheating on their sales results input. The house was divided and not even the mail in your mail slot or the printing on the printer was safe. Frank suggested a team building event. The teams unanimously agreed on going to a bar. It snowed that day and only a fraction of the team showed up. Everyone drank like fish and talked about their DUI's. I was shocked how many people on the team had had a DUI. The attitude toward Frank was spreading to my team too. Frank had other problems in Des Moines where he had inherited a contentious situation between two sales managers. His absence in Minnesota gave a great bit of time for dissent to foment. Mickey became the lynch pin. He was as helpful as he could be to anyone on my team who asked, but he was sure to give them his opinion of Frank and me. He painted a picture that working for Nick was much better, and that Nick's team was more respected.

This is what it looks like when it is broken. And it is broken in a lot of places. The question is how do you fix it? There was no room for anyone to ignore the problem. Everyone's job was on the line. A 'shut up and sell' mentality would not cut it. An active campaign of mud-slinging meant that if you did not throw mud back, you might be pegged as the cause of the problem or torn to pieces by your own side for not assisting in the battle against the other team. The insane thing was that no one, not one person, quit to take a job elsewhere during this period. Many of the people who were laid off the previous fall had been hired by our chief competitor across town. When they heard about the environment, most felt happy they were no longer here. They could not understand an office at war with itself. As public as the feud was on the sales floor, no one breathed a word about the environment to Loni, least of all Nick or I. It was obvious that this was some sort of failure in leadership, and for the life of me I could not understand what I was doing wrong.

In retrospect, it is obvious to me that I should have left at that point. I had an option to try my leadership skills elsewhere or go back to a sales role. I kick myself for becoming so embroiled in that mess that

I actually wanted to stick around to see what might happen next. As long as I was part of the next phase, I would claim victory. But living to fight another day in a situation like that was clearly nothing more than a waste of time. It was time lost that could never be recaptured. Although the lesson was learned the first day, like the character in the movie, 'Groundhog Day', I was reliving it over and over every day. I finally had that day nailed by the following fall.

Another October and another layoff looming...the familiar unease of am I 'safe' or not. I met Frank at his condo a day before the new roster was announced. I sat and listened to him talking to a team member who was concerned about losing her job. The ones who get released usually know who they will be. They call, looking for the 'governor's reprieve' at the last minute. That never happens. They keep talking to feel comforted. After the call, Frank and I talk about business. He asks if I want to talk about the layoffs.

"Not really," I tell him. He looks relieved and he agrees he doesn't want to discuss it either.

'Heads will roll day' comes and goes. Somehow, I find myself as the last remaining sales manager in Minnesota. What was left of my old team from the Small Markets days is now gone, and all my old peers now are reporting to me. I am not feeling as glib as I eat my celebratory steak and fries lunch alone. The lunch is feeling more like a last supper. I ask myself why I am worrying. I beat out Nick and now the group that was fighting has been whittled down to one team (largely made up of Nick's old team), all reporting to me. I know there will be some difficult personalities to deal with, but I know how to hold out the olive branch.

I am old hat at this people management by now. Before I leave for the day and start my holiday senseless spending, and maybe take a hot shower and not turn off the water mid-stream, I stop in to see Frank. He is all business and says all the normal things, "I hate these layoffs, but if we don't perform, we need to expect them." I agree, but I want to talk about my situation. Somehow, I can't bring myself to asking. I figure we are in this together. Like two peas in a pod.

The January sales kick-off is slightly different at my company. Based on our size, many of the direct sellers are not at the actual event. Their management comes, and management is expected to pass on the material for a successful 20XX! We have two solid days of listening to our leaders tell us about enhancements for the new year, along with incentives and quota arrangements that aim to please. New investment is touted and our CEO even stops in to give us a quick state of the business address. Her address always ends with the importance of our business sales team. Between sessions, the regional vice presidents act as the larger orbital bodies around which people congregate for shelter and safety. Braver individuals look for managers they have worked with in the past or old friends they have made during long tenures with the company. I search out the people who are smoking and not talking on the phone. These are the international employees. Their teams and customers are already asleep and their taboos around smoking have not yet hit prime time. I avoid Loni and my team at all costs. This is probably not a good move, but I figure they won't miss me. I look at the sea of people and the regional vice president satellites. This could be a giant job fair where the contestants are trying to keep their positions through the next year's round of layoffs. I desperately look for anyone new to talk to. I see a guy I know from marketing. He smiles and walks away. I am too low on the totem pole for him. I nearly bump into Ethan at the snack table. "How ya doin' buddy?" He calls everyone buddy. His eyes begin to scan the horizon. I know I need to make my pitch quick. I stammer aloud boasting on my results and how much I enjoyed working under him. "Hey, listen, I see some guys over here I need to talk to. You be good." He walks away giving me less time than I believe decent in a fishbowl like this. I wander into the auditorium. TotalCom has hired a comedian for the nightly entertainment. He makes a mistake and tells the same joke twice inside a minute. He falls out of character and apologizes. He says, "That has never happened to me before." The show goes on, but it isn't very funny anymore.

I want out. Out of my current situation, out of this company's grip. But I don't know which way to turn. I have no elevator speech that would give anyone any reason to believe I wasn't just another 30 year paycheck guy. I turn in before the bar becomes a circus tent of stupidity. I am always surprised how willing some people are to drink heavily around their co-workers. Our old segment head, Curtis, (the hulking guy who scared Loni many years ago), liked to close the bar with his sales team. I watched him do it from my hotel room above the pool bar at the Ritz in Mexico when I was at Royalty Club in 2006.

Back at the kick-off, I call my wife from my hotel room. I cannot let out my frustration because I am afraid someone will hear me complaining through the walls of the Hilton. I hang up and lay on the bed. I start wondering whether they can tap my thoughts. I quickly turn off the light and close my eyes.

After the closing session I catch a cab back to the Las Vegas airport with Loni. Lucky me. Loni is always looking to model thrift and I happen to be standing at the wrong place at the wrong time. I wave goodbye to the throng of Loni's well-wishers from around the Midwest as the cab door closes. Idle conversation commences about the Nevada landscape and how cold it is going to be when we get back to Minnesota. Loni doesn't want to talk shop lest the non-English speaking cab driver may make an inside trade and change his pitiful fortune. I go along with Loni, the Queen of careful; the 30 year paycheck woman par ex-cellence. At the airport, Loni invites me to have a drink and some appetizers at the bar near the gate. We will be splitting the bill surgically. I see some of the Detroit team walk by. Loni waives but does not beckon them to join us. I figure it is time to level with Loni. I tell her I want to continue to grow at the company and would like to experience new things. I let her know I am even willing to move. I can see in her eyes that she has very different ideas and plans for me. This is the woman who gave the nod for me to attend those Royalty Clubs and she always loved my sales efforts. She supported me in her own way. It doesn't dawn on me that she possibly could have felt miffed by my departure to work with Frank in small markets. It seems obvious that anyone would take a promotion working for someone they know and like, but I don't think Loni completely understood.

Inside the large organization, everyone lives in a bubble. That bubble includes you and other people who see things as you do. Recently, I was speaking with a vice president who was bemoaning the management style at her company. The miraculous thing was that she claimed not to be part of the problem. It wasn't her fault! Or her boss, who she thinks is fabulous. It is the fault of the hierarchy! That is what needs to change. She continued that since there is no practical way to accomplish that, we just need to 'stay in the swim lanes' when dealing with problems. That means protect the hierarchy by protecting the people in your bubble.

When I heard this, I took a deep breath and asked myself, 'If I don't believe I am part of the problem, and this regional vice president doesn't feels she is part of the problem, where exactly does the problem lie?' Whatever the actual answer is, it is never the person you are talking to. Convenient. You either have power over that person or they have power over you. They either like you or they don't. They either see you as part of their success or not. In a command-and-control structure, the lines are always black and white. This reduces the stress of trying to honestly know where you stand. You stand wherever the machine says you stand. It can be very comforting because you are never unsure. Another executive director was complaining to me recently about his boss. She was sending him mixed signals. This created a lot of stress. "Honestly, I did not know whether I was going to be fired or praised when I got up each morning." This sinking feeling is the enemy of structure and structure means security. To know that you honestly don't know if you are on the right path is the beginning of a liberation that can take you anywhere your ideas desire.

Minneapolis Act II

I have been told to sit in the corner by so many vice presidents I have already lost count. The odd thing is that every interaction I have had with a true executive has been a reasonably positive one. It has been one where my ideas were validated and in some cases used and acted upon. I wonder whether this hierarchy we follow actually only exists in our collective consciousness. No one wants to own it, but everyone perpetuates its existence. Perhaps the easiest way to stamp it out is as simple as turning on the light and finding out that this evil monster does not lurk under the bed after all.

I totally misread Loni at the airport bar. This is typical of most of our interactions. We munch on fries and she smiles as I tell her I would like to discuss my career with her. She seems happy to oblige and encourages me to set up some time on her calendar. Conversations with her have never been easy for me. Do you have people in your life with whom you just don't seem to communicate well? It is as if the translator software is not working. Whatever you say is misconstrued and whatever the other person says seems abrasive and untrue. You find your head going up and down vaguely agreeing with each other. Loni was like that for me. Since the beginning of that year, I had attended her leadership call on Friday mornings. These two hour marathon calls are a touch point for her entire region. Everyone who is not in Minneapolis has a chance to multitask on the call, but we lucky ones in Minnesota are expected to be in Loni's conference room in person. The call starts with each team manually giving its forecast for new sales. Loni uses a calculator and a pad of paper to plot her fortune based on that information. She is generally inscrutable during this.".'m, kay", her favorite filler response.

Sometimes, if she is short on her numbers for the month and someone has vastly backed off on a previously high forecast, she explodes. Next, each sales manager goes through his or her top opportunities for the week giving a blow by blow description in tedious detail of what they have been up to. This often devolves into a rationalizing for their very existence with Loni. Once in a while she gets ornery and blasts someone's thinking or approach. The response is always silence, since (at least during these meetings) she is the smartest person in the room.

A couple weeks later in Minneapolis, at the appointed time, Loni is ready for our career conversation. Her desk is empty and spotless in keeping with some unwritten rule of being an executive. The rule says whoever visits your office needs to know you are important because of the ease at which you do all the many wonderful things you do. It has a different effect on me. I wonder what she actually does all day.

Loni is a very structured executive. One thing she liked to do was visit all her branches in alphabetical order each quarter. Each quarter she scheduled a visit to each city under her jurisdiction. The sales teams were expected to tell their clients that the big cheese was in town and schedule appointments for her with the customer's executives. The reputation of a branch and the understanding of how well a branch was functioning depended in large measure on a productive and well-choreographed visit. The branch vice presidents spend a lot of time making sure these visits go well and that the right image is portrayed. For us in Minneapolis, we saw Loni each day...in the elevator, grabbing a slice of pizza for lunch, taking the elevator down to her heated, indoor reserved parking spot under the building...a perk of her pay grade. Loni did not organize a visit to the Minnesota branch since the psychology of setting appointments for the big cheese coming into town was moot. She lived in the Twin Cities. Because of her involvement in the community and her long tenure, most of the business leaders knew who she was. For her, this was not a bright spot for getting appointments. Loni knew how to fill the bill as a confident leader from a Fortune 500 company, but, like a prophet in her own country, she did not have many endearing relationships with executives around town. It is peculiar how customers expect a local executive to help them more than one who has just 'flown in.' People figure a visitor from out of town is busy. She must be out of town a lot, so there is no expectation that she can roll up her sleeves and help everyone, everywhere. Whereas if the executive lives in town, the question becomes what is she doing each day to help solve my problems? Loni had this working against her. Her local relationships were virtually non-existent. This meant that we took her on very few appointments each year. She defiantly threw her busy appointment schedule in other Midwest cities in our face and asked us, "Why can't you get me more appointments in Minneapolis?" I was honestly trying to answer that question.

Loni came out from behind her desk and offered me a seat at her small round table. This was supposed to trigger a feeling of equality, collegiality and empathy. It is something most people with large offices have learned over the years. The image of her deigning to come down from behind her large, paperless oak desk only sent a signal to me that I was less than she was and I had better not construe this as a time for any silly egalitarian talk.

I told Loni I was ready to move on. I did it as nicely as I could. I agreed that there was a lot to do with the new team, but maybe that challenge was best saved for someone new. I had my go at it, and I had been successful.

Loni was ready for me. "What was it that you wanted to do next?" she asked.

This is an old trick to get rid of someone who just wants out of a job. It quickly gauges whether a subordinate is running away from or towards a new situation. It worked on me. I was clearly running away, anywhere was better than here. In response to Loni's questions I stammered like a school kid. I listed, in the most general way possible, positions I thought I would be good at. I said things like, 'marketing director' and 'product director'. I let her know that I was fishing for a promotion in all of this, not a lateral move. Loni laughed and said,

"Kid, I am going to give you some sage advice." As it turns out, this is the same advice she gives everyone aggressively looking to move up.

"I call it Loni's principle of promotion. You always need to move laterally first. What I mean is you cannot move out of a current role into a new one and expect a promotion at the same time. You are unknown wherever you move. You will need to prove yourself if you want to move up."

The message was simple: if you want to move up right away, it will have to be under my watch. Otherwise, you can move your family on your own dime for a lateral position to a different group and slog it out there for a few more years and hope they like you enough to give you a promotion. Loni pushed her chair back a few inches and crossed her legs as if to punctuate her advice with a "Good luck with that."

Loni looked satisfied, as if she had just moved her queen into a position to checkmate my king. We sat looking at each other for what seemed like minutes. Then she walked to her computer and started reading out job postings her peers around the country send her. It seemed that many others also turned to her for sage advice and recommendations. "International operations director". 'I'd do that', I thought. The list went on, there was nothing that sounded too bad. But as she walked back to the table, I could see she wasn't going to help me move. Seeing she had me wrapped tightly around her finger, she raised an eyebrow. I had to do something. I told her that I felt I had the sales manager job figured out and I just wanted to move onto something more challenging. This triggered her ire. She laughed and pointed at me, "You think you have it figured out, do you? Not even close." She sneered, "You think you had some success in small markets and that is the same as middle markets. Those are two different shows. Those are two different animals. Now, I can tell you there are sales managers who have it figured out and are ready for a new assignment, but not you."

I lost my cool: "Can you give me an example of someone in the region who does have it fig-ured out?"

"Ned in Sioux City." Ned? Really? Ned had been in a sales manager job since I first began with the company thirteen years ago. He was easily the most obsequious and sycophantic manager on our weekly calls. He was always calling out how all his success stemmed from Loni's excellent leadership. Additionally, Ned was waging a private war with the other sales manager in Iowa. Ned had been passed over for countless promotions and was nearing the corporate tipping point.

The tipping point is a magical place that mid-level managers find themselves in usually when they approach their late forties. It is a realization that they aren't going to be able to get promoted fast enough to become an executive director, much less a vice president. They are running out of time before they reach an age where they are no longer going to be considered for promotions. Logically, they retrench and swallow the news. Then they slog on, only without their ambition. They put family, friends and anything else in front of their work. They work hard enough to be viewed as valuable in the role they have and hope to heck that role survives market changes before they reach retirement age. Some people call it 'retired in position' and many leaders see these employees as some of their best. They are the ones worth protecting. They will never challenge the status quo and have no ambition that could make a leader look bad for rewarding them. A deep cynicism often accompanies someone who reaches the tipping point. They no longer expect fairness or equitable treatment and preach that new gospel to their teams. They rely on a hope they can maximize commissions to accelerate an early retirement.

They no longer care if they remain on a list of 'high-potential' employees. 'High-potential' employees are the list of 'promotables'. Being on a list like that can make you feel as if that promotion is just around the corner. It can also make you feel safe. After all, who was going to let a 'high-potential' employee go? That would be crazy? You are safe as houses on the 'promotable' list even if you never were going to be considered for a promotion. I was on the 'high-potential' list. It didn't help me. More importantly, it didn't save me when the time came for changes. Sure, I got to keep a job, but I wasn't going over the tipping point without a fight. For all I know, Ned is still on the 'high-potential' list. Last I heard, he had gone past the tipping point as was expected.

Loni's final act in our three part meeting was to give me a book called *The Speed of Trust* By Stephen Covey Jr. I want to be sure to say that this is a fine piece of business literature, endorsed and lauded by many fine minds. However, it was also the "Christmas Book" that year. A Christmas Book is given each year by the executive manager to her direct reports. It is a subtle way of directing culture and building a common experience for far flung teams. The executive can use the book to generate dialog on innovating and improving culture, and the author is usually more than happy to sell a program by which this conversation can take place. Usually that conversation comes in the form of a $100,000 workshop at a suitably comfortable executive retreat center. Loni thought the book would help me build relationships with my new team. Perhaps she also hoped that I would learn to head past the tipping point and fall in line like Ned. I promised to read it. Loni then offered to meet with me quarterly to continue our discussion. She opened her door and I saw myself out. I walked to the elevator bank. 'The Speed of Trust', I thought. The doors closed and the elevator began to descend.

Becoming more transparent at work was my latest obsession. The Covey book was inspiring me to try new things. How else could I change the status quo if I was going to rebuild. One thing I tried to do differently was email. I got so many messages that I simply deleted each day without reading. It seemed like a full time job just deleting email and it really seemed quite absurd. I thought about a John Paul Sartre sequel to "No Exit" that I would entitle "No Delete Key". But Covey convinced me to put down my cynical ideas for a moment and really look at the situation. People were sending me tons of messages that they thought a Sales Manager should see. By deleting them, I was simply perpetuating (maybe even increasing) the number of messages I got. If I didn't read the messages, I reasoned, then the senders would eventually find out. They wanted validation as much as anyone else. I decided to experiment with reading cover to cover every email I got for one week. I got hopelessly behind doing this, but I did learn a lot. I had been missing out on a number of interesting things. New tools, websites and webinars were being rolled out constantly. One such initiative was a webinar series on social media. I signed for it as my inbox slowly filled to bursting.

Social media was not unknown to me. I had a LinkedIn profile and a Facebook page, although I didn't do much networking that way. I had never heard of Twitter until the webinar and I was instantly intrigued.

Meanwhile, my email box was getting more and more full. Normally, I would be deleting like crazy, but an experiment was an experiment, and I had another couple of days to go until I could say I read every message that came my way for an entire work week. My blood pressure was rising, though. Then it dawned on me. I started wondering if I could reduce email somehow by using social media. How might a Twitter account allow me to connect better with my team? Would a Twitter web link instead of a four page email in my inbox allow me to digest information more efficiently? My mind was swirling with ideas. It was amazing the kinds of things I was learning from the email I never looked at previously.

After the webinar, I signed up for a Twitter account and started poking around. What were people saying about TotalCom on Twitter? What were people saying about our customers? But the more I searched, the more I got an entirely different idea. I was astounded how quickly I could digest information that came in 140 character blurbs. I felt like I woke up Evelyn Wood, the esteemed speed reader, from the dead inside my brain. Finding interesting information on a topic was a snap and it was so easy to ignore the superfluous. Best of all, on Twitter there is no need to hit a delete key. A spark lit in my head. Every problem I heard from my team, from being overloaded by emails and messages to trying to get customers signed up for events and webinars, all of it could be answered by social media. Promoting customer events would be a hundred times easier via Twitter. I signed up for all the social media webinars and began deleting email as quickly as I could. In my role as sales manager, I hated forwarding emails to my team with small action items that I then needed to follow up on and track. But this is one of the primary roles of a TotalCom middle manager—making sure employees are in compliance. My metrics and effectiveness for getting my team to report their forecasts, be accurate with that forecast and complete their customer surveys on time was almost as important as selling things and helping to make our sales plan. Executives like Loni saw the selling part as cyclical and market and economy driven. Operational soundness was something the team could control and was a leading indicator for everything else from her perspective. From my point of view, so many of the operational tasks could be automated and more time could be given back to selling. Later, TotalCom would hire a large management consulting team to come in and say the same thing. Giving more time back to sales people to sell would become a rallying cry for years after. Time wasting internal reporting was a top complaint from my team and something I wanted to help with using social media. One idea I had was to create an internal Twitter system that would allow each individual to get short messages outlining key compliance actions. It would be easy to read and easily digestible and it would not bog down the email inbox. It could even be viewed on a smartphone.

There was an innovation system at TotalCom that "crowd sourced" ideas. Crowd sourcing allows anyone to post an idea in a shared database for everyone to review. At TotalCom, ideas were categorized as either money saving or increasing topline revenue. The tool logged the ideas and put a timer on them. Inside of a defined timeline they needed to meet certain requirements otherwise they were deleted. For example, each idea needed twenty 'likes' inside the first month and five reviews inside the first sixty days. From there ideas were bubbled up to the next level of management where more reviews were done. Eventually, the best ideas made it to the top, executives discussed the merit of each and the very best ideas received funding. The other interesting part about the platform was investor bucks which were earned for giving reviews. These bucks in turn could be used to 'fund' ideas in later stages of development, like a venture capital firm funds a new business.

But I am not a true believer in crowd funding, crowd sourcing or crowd anything else for that that matter. People invent things for many reasons. And consumers vote for new ideas by buying them, but only if the new inventions are useful to them. The TotalCom crowd sourcing system provided a mini-market inside the company to test out concepts in advance of seeing whether it made sense to manufacture and sell these new products and services. But there are three problems with this approach.

First, things that sound like good ideas are not always good ideas. Sometimes a simple idea seems like it would be just the thing to solve a problem, but when it comes down to it, there really isn't that much value. A good example of this is almost anything you see being sold on late night broadcast TV. Once I saw an enormous bag and vacuum that attached to your riding mower to pick up leaves in autumn. It looked ideal for the job, but the fact is that picking up leaves using a blower or rake and bag is not that much more difficult and certainly a huge metal add-on to the mower is not worth the expense, storage and hassle of this contraption. Otherwise, you would see one on every suburban lawn during the fall.

The second reason is the Homer Simpson effect. In a 1991 Simpson's cartoon, Danny DeVito is the voice of Homer's brother who is an auto executive in Detroit. He is trying to make America great again by building a car that will be more desirable to the American public than foreign models. He hires Homer to design it. Homer opts for lots of cup holders, gadgets and bling that will make him feel important and good. But the car is a flop because it gets terrible gas mileage and the lack of function over form makes the car unusable. My point is that sometimes the crowds know less about making something useful than a well-trained engineer who has studied design and function over the years.

The final problem is that we cannot protect ourselves from ourselves. What I mean is that wherever there are people, there are egos and the need to feel important. The innovation system slowly filled over time with trolls of different stripes. First, there were "Phantoms of the Opera" who had been wronged by having their idea bashed and thus their dreams dashed by other trolls. They vowed for revenge and now spent time accumulating points to throw their weight and votes around in flaming other's ideas. They will argue the finer points of a beautiful idea. Their goal is that no one ever wins because they didn't. Meanwhile, "Egotist" trolls bash ideas with long flowing reviews that serve to keep others from validating an idea even if they like it. No one wants to touch something that has been flamed with such vitriol by one of these haters for fear that the same hater will somehow take out revenge on them.

The whole thing often boils down to a popularity contest, but it cost you your friends and your entire day's work in trying to keep your idea properly protected from trolls that lurk along the path and asking for favorable reviews by anyone who owes you a favor.

I did work very hard to get my idea of a private Twitter promoted and, in retrospect, the idea wasn't really stellar. It was dashed against the rocks of Troll Bay by a spirited and notorious Phantom of the Opera who worked in a technical role in Indianapolis. I tried not to be bitter. What had I learned? This was the new me from The Speed of Trust

Book, trying to learn lessons from my failures. I came to this conclusion. The next good idea I had, I wasn't going to bring to this market. Rather I was going to take it to the real world. My idea came several years later in the form of another social media innovation that allowed companies to privately create a 'like' button on internal documents and emails. The 'like' feature allowed employees to win clout points that in turn could be used by human resources to give objective, merit-based raises and promotions. It is a 'publish or perish' writ large in the corporate world. I sent this idea along with $350 to the US patent office. As of 6/15/2014, it is still a provisional patent being examined for final approval. I would rather face the trolls of the real world market who will vote with their pocketbooks than the internal trolls who want to pass on their inner pain.

Chapter 10

A brief Interlude: The bar or 'We'll go for one quick one'

Bob took a job with the small business group in November. He came from a major competitor of TotalCom's. Bob played football at the University of Iowa River City and his voice was as big and booming as his stature. Bob was a no nonsense kind of guy....a salesman's salesman. Our cubes were adjacent and because of our mutual loud voices, at any given time, we both knew exactly what the other was doing. I never get angry with loud talkers, because surely I have been the annoying loud talker on the airplane, at the restaurant or in the office dozens and dozens of times. To all of you whom I have annoyed: I am truly sorry.

Bob was constantly on the go with his new clients who were based mainly in the western suburbs. But, like me, he lived in the east metro and often found himself at his desk at the end of the day. We both had wives at home with a baby, so we avoided heading home until the last possible moment. I have never enjoyed the relative stress free nature of the office in the late afternoon as much as when my children were tiny. By doing more work, I also felt I was girding myself against future job insecurity. Staying late was a weapon I was using to keep my family safe. What I was really doing was avoiding the tough work at home.

THE 30 YEAR PAYCHECK

The whole notion seems ridiculous now. More hours on the job never seemed to get anyone anywhere. It is purposeful hours that hold the biggest advantage to any human endeavor. One afternoon around 4.30 pm, the office was nearly empty except for Bob and me. We were chatting over the cubes. He had noticed that Key's, the breakfast and lunch joint across the street from our building, was now running a two for one happy hour. Let's go down there and check it out! He convinced me and we went for a beer. The price was right, and it was good to get out. Bob even dropped me off in St Paul on his way back to the eastern burbs, which saved me the bus fare. But, more importantly, we got to discuss work. The topics were everything my wife couldn't understand and didn't want to try to pick up on after a long day at home with our daughter. Bob and I slurped down our beers and discussed customers, problems and the inner workings of office politics.

We began to get together regularly at Keys and the cadence and discussion was always the same. Two beers and a healthy dose of venting and listening. Sometimes we spoke about things at home, but for me that was never as interesting. I deemed these meetings as cathartic at the time. They were keeping me sane in the cut-throat environment of a sagging-balloon technology industry where the only thing that was certain was a yearly layoff.

Layoffs are rarely random. I would like to think the one I went through at OneGlobe was, but it wasn't. Two businesses had merged and the controlling party wanted its own-- and it kept them. I survived countless layoffs at TotalCom by constantly and consistently performing and fitting into the culture just enough that I was always seen as someone they would miss. I got my training and expense reports done on time and I always found the 'extra sale' when the sales center was short at the end of the month. I figured time at the bar would enable me to bite my lip better because I had a place to vent about anything negative happening in the office.

The people at Keys knew us by name after a few years. We celebrated the holidays, key sales, and birthdays at that place. We often brought guests to our sessions, but Bob and I were always the Mayor and Fire Chief at Keys, holding court. The Global business sales vice president sometimes showed up. He always drank alone and he was always the last to leave, assuming that he ever did. He was a mixed blessing. He bought us drinks and spun fine tales about upper management leaders he worked with. But his stories got dull after an hour and he would always prod us to stay longer than we wanted.

I asked myself why I felt dread when we saw the Global VP walking over to our table. After all, he gave us a glimpse into circles above our stature. He even had the inside skinny on layoffs and reorganization announcements. I started wondering if the time spent in the bar was at all time well spent for my career. What was I working out? Was I just wasting emotional energy slogging through the problems and politics I needed to face each day anyway? Or was I supporting my friend and vice versa in our daily grind and journey?

Bob faced a major personal struggle with his family that I don't think I could have made it through with any semblance of sanity. During those extremely dark days, I was there for him. Two other sales people,

Randy and Annie, often came along. Complaint sessions lasted later and later. More and more pressure mounted at work.

Once I became a sales manager, a few more reorganizations found Bob, Randy and Annie reporting to me. Despite the changed relationship, we still met at Keys. If the Global VP could come down alone and spin tales all evening, what was so wrong with me hanging out with my old friends? Of course, the Global VP was an alcoholic. Over three years, I watched all three of my bar friends get laid off. The hundreds of beers and mountains of paper that would have comprised our transcripted conversations couldn't change anything or make it any easier.

A few months before Bob was laid off, we were down in Bloomington for a meeting. After the meeting we went to a nearby bar. Bob and I left at the same time and I was following him back to the interstate. It was my daughter's birthday and a Friday evening. Bob got ahead of me at a stoplight and when I entered the ramp after him, I saw his car off to the side of the road. He had rear-ended the guy in front of him. Thankfully no one was hurt. The police arrived but luckily nothing came of it. I stood in the dark with Bob atop a compacted snow bank as the officer filled out the paperwork and Bob worried they would check his breath. I missed my daughter's birthday party because I needed to give Bob a ride home. His van was totaled.

Intimate, frequent meetings can inspire small groups to revolution and innovation, but this one certainly did not. It could have changed things, but it didn't. Instead everyone reported their problems and spent time hearing everyone else's. I don't remember a plan ever developing from these meetings that made a difference the next day. It was a meet-

A brief Interlude: The bar or 'We'll go for one quick one'

ing of the prisoners inside the maximum security prison.   It was hopeless. There was no way out. Stitch by stitch I was sewing the orange
jumpsuit onto my skin.

Chapter 11

Minnesota Act III

I began my story describing the day my boss, Frank, who had protected me from the sometimes merciless corporate machine, told me he was leaving...and not taking me with him. Frank had done something about his situation. He made a change. He called on his network and found a job running a group of technical specialists. He was Mickey's new boss. He would still be involved with our sales branch, but reported to someone other than Loni. While he did not explain it to me at the time, he was enacting Loni's patented move-laterally-in-order-to-move-up maneuver. Frank was still ambitious and he wasn't going to let a bad environment bring him down. Personally, I was fine with that, but why didn't he find a way for me to come along with him? I still expected him to save me from my dilemma and ultimately from myself.

In the end, our destiny belongs to nobody but us. Even favors and help from others often directly results from the work we do each day. Getting out of bed early is the first step. Spending our time productively is the second. I was having difficulty with both. I was having trouble hauling myself out of bed. Once I eventually made it to the office, most of my days were spent primarily feeling sorry for myself.

A few days later, Frank gave me more details. His replacement would be announced in the coming weeks, but he was fairly sure it was going to be Rhonda. I first met Rhonda when I came back from the Netherlands. She was a new hire in global markets, having come from a successful stretch at a competitor. But back then she was low person on the totem pole. I am not a big fan of luck or fate, but Rhonda certainly rose up from interesting circumstances. She had been placed on a litany of down-trodden accounts. One was a regional electronics retailer. She did her job and built strong relationships despite the bone dry sales funnels and minimal prospect of selling anything. But the economy was changing. The retailer hit a growth spurt and Rhonda was perfectly situated to capitalize on it. Her success was phenomenal and the account grew to become one of the largest in our region. With that came accolades, exposure and a succession of promotions. While I worked my international medical device company for everything it was worth, Rhonda moved straight past me on an effortless escalator to the top. She now had a team of people working for her to support this mammoth account. She later told me she really did not want the job as Frank's replacement, but was urged by the top brass (above Loni) to take it. The region, especially Minneapolis, was in a shambles and everyone counseled her that it had no place to go but up.

This put me in a precarious position. Rhonda had little experience in running a sales center and would rely on her boss Loni for suggestions on what to do. There is no doubt that although Rhonda would be running several sales centers in the Midwest, Loni was painting a bull's eye over Minneapolis. Loni wanted to see change and she wanted to see it happen quickly. In a classical sense, I was left holding the bag. There was no one left to blame but me. A few weeks after the announcement about Rhonda, I was dragging in the trash cans from the curb in front of my house. One tipped over and I began violently kicking it. In the snow, cold and dark of a Minnesota winter under the sulfur street lamps, I could be seen kicking a trashcan until I couldn't feel my feet inside my badly scuffed work shoes. I am not a violent or angry person, but I felt betrayed by the safety net and the promise of continuous upward mobility. Rhonda was indifferent toward me. She knew the drill and managed Loni expectations and desires, not mine. Probably at Loni's suggestion, she interviewed my entire team one by one in private. This made me feel uneasy, but she told me she just wanted to assist with any changes that needed to be made. She was guarded with disclosing what she had learned from them. I cannot think of anything that could give my team a greater signal that it was time for a revolution against me than these one-on-one interviews. I eventually heard that she was asking their opinions on what was and wasn't working in Minneapolis. Mickey got wind of all this and began running coaching sessions for the more malleable minds on what to tell Rhonda. It couldn't have been flattering for me. Mickey also made an end run with Loni, describing to her what he thought the problem was. To sum it up, it was me. I tried to remind Rhonda that many people on the team had only reported to me for a couple of months. But I could do nothing to stop the onslaught. I called Frank incessantly to get his advice. He lived out his fantasies by urging me to fire everybody.

Three months flew by and I found myself back in Loni's office with my next coaching session. I painted as happy a picture as possible on how things were going, but Loni smelled blood in the water.

"I hear from Rhonda you are having problems controlling the team."

THE 30 YEAR PAYCHECK

I bristled. Our results had actually improved over the past few months. But results often improve right after a new leader is hired. It has everything to do with fear of being fired. Kicking up the results for the new boss is an insurance policy against the fall layoffs. By proving to the new boss that you can do the job, you will fare better in the fall stack ranking. But Loni was drawing a circle around my failings. I tried to gently push back on the accusations. I knew that Rhonda was not her choice as the new Branch Manager and I played to that. I indicated that some of what she was hearing was a result of Frank leaving. Loni was having none of it. She probably felt snubbed by Frank's walking away and she wasn't going to have someone at my level try to play the same trick on her. Next, I had the pleasure of hearing Loni's sage advice on how she managed her first team three decades ago. She told me that she had been too strict at first and learned over time to be more evenhanded. She recommended a few more dreadful books that I dutifully read, "The 7 Minute Manager" and other titles you no doubt read or heard of two decades ago. As Loni spoke, I could hear the voice of my former Vice President, Ethan, echoing in my ears: "If you tell me everything is ok, and there is still a problem, I will assume you are the problem."

The walls kept closing in, but I went on the offensive. I did what any good corporate employee would do and built a PowerPoint deck outlining the strengths and weakness of each of my team members and my plans on how to develop each one. This deck had very little of me in it-- and a lot of Loni. I figured if I managed like Loni did, I could fit in better and survive to get a better job. Besides, Loni had to retire soon and there were rumors that it would even be this year. Fat chance. We had just lapped 2008 and the hole in the stock market was now anchoring a large number of aging baby boomers in their retired-in-place jobs.

I got Frank's input and endorsement on the PowerPoint and presented it to Rhonda. In the PowerPoint, I identified 'keepers' and 'potentials' for replacing based on results and attitude. Rhonda would neither agree nor disagree with me, making it all the more uncomfortable and confusing.

Mickey saw what was happening and was ready for his revenge. Once again, the plan centered squarely on pushing me down the stairs. Mickey had befriended one of my failing reps and was going on all his sales calls. Mickey is an excellent sales person and his engagement was making a difference. The cost of Mickey's involvement was allegiance to him. My new concentration on managing Rhonda and being operationally impeccable to mirror Loni's expectations had taken me away from going on sales calls and knowing what was happening at my customers. Meanwhile, I was getting fewer and fewer invitations from my team to go out on sales calls with them. I realized that there were large customers of some of the new people on my team I had never met. I thought back to the boycott of bringing out Frank to these customers the year before and an itching paranoia overcame me. During weekly reviews with my team, I requested meetings with these new clients. My requests were met with resistance. Somewhere on the sales floor, Mickey was smirking. I squelched every excuse and started making headway, to the chagrin of many of the reps. In some cases I set up the meetings directly. I am sure the customers were puzzled by my calls, but I wasn't going to be denied these meetings. The salespeople did not appreciate my actions. I tried to respond by being helpful to them in making new sales with these clients, but they resented me more than ever for assuming they wanted or needed help. One of the blind spots was that I was now managing them the way Loni was managing me. Weekly reviews were more focused on numbers and moving red to green on the myriad of spreadsheets that constituted 'results' to executives. I was no longer inspirational and no one would confuse me with the guy who took a sales team from last place to first just a few years before.

It didn't matter. I began to sour on the team and I was running frantically to leave the job at all costs with as much of my pride and career intact as possible. Mickey continued to work his charm, and another failing rep bought it hook line and sinker. Mickey told him I was not long for the world in my current job and associating with me would only be a liability. For all I knew, he predicted he would be my successor. One evening, I asked the rep to take me to one of his clients. He flatly refused. I documented the situation by coaxing him to refuse again in email. I stewed on 6th street waiting for the 94 bus to take me home to St Paul. Next morning I phoned human resources and said I wanted to put the rep on 'an improvement plan'.

In our business an 'improvement plan' is a nice way of saying that you are going to be let go and probably have four months at the most to find a new job. My very glib explanation to Rhonda was that this sort of insubordination would never help us get better in Minneapolis. This rep was not going to help us improve, and having him around set a bad example for everyone else. A few months later, I collected his laptop and corporate card and shook his hand good-bye. I checked the box on the human resource file entitled: 'Do not rehire'. The rest of the team went into a tailspin. My point was made. I was not only a minion of Loni and her management by spreadsheet style, I was now her executioner reigning by terror. I hated myself for this. Why was I listening to Loni? Where was the old me? What was I doing? I was having even more trouble getting out of bed, and the specter of the 2001 OneGlobe layoff loomed large. I rationalized that I needed to follow Loni's way. It would only be for a bit more and then she would retire or would help me get a new job. One thing was for sure-- doing it my way would only put me in greater peril. I buried myself behind a version of myself that I thought could get me out of this situation. Where I was going was a total mystery to me. I just knew I needed to get out of this burning building and take refuge on the sidewalk under a fireman's blanket for a little while.

Meanwhile, at corporate headquarters, a new cult was being built. It was based on the age old theory of 'rhetoric' and was reassembled by an enterprising training company. This training program had caught the eye and budget of TotalCom. At the sales kick-off in January, we had heard that a new training dubbed the Science of Selling was coming our way and the entire global sales force would be trained in the coming months. What is more, the training company was determined not to make this a 'one and done' session, and sold TotalCom on the need to incorporate the 'scientific principles' of the program into everything we do. This included new product training, account team reviews and reviews of top opportunities with upper management. The four letter acronym HEAT (Hear, Engage, Ask, Tell), was the basis of the program and would find its way into everything I did for the next several months.

There was a sales manager training that took Loni, Rhonda and me to Milwaukee. Loni suggested we synchronize hotels and flights and we spent that entire week together eating breakfast, lunch and dinner at the same table. Loni loved to play a game where we would all try to come as close to our per diem as possible. At dinner we pulled out our receipts to see what we had spent so far for lunch and breakfast, and calculated how much we had as a group to spend on dinner. Then we found an economical bottle of wine and an appetizer to try to fill each person's gap. That week Loni talked a lot about her financial planner. I listened intently for any signs that she might retire soon. None were there. We turned in each night around 8 pm. I went to the gym, swam and sorted through email. I wondered what Loni was up to. She didn't bring her laptop. Each morning she regaled us with a fine digest of commercial television from the night before.

I enjoyed the training and became good friends with the trainer. I thought that the training had a lot of good ideas and suggestions as to how our sales force could really improve. On my team, everyone just worked an individual 'tried and true' style with varying degrees of success. Preparing for meetings and sales campaigns with a sense of purpose made a lot of sense to me. It was something that we almost never did. The week in training went by tediously. At the end of the week, we had a final exam that we self-graded. This means each of us graded our neighbor. Loni slid down a few seats from me, but I peaked at her grade on the final. She barely passed. I aced it. It had been snowing all morning and it was coming down in enormous flakes that were consuming the roads as we sped to the airport. Loni invited Rhonda and me to the Skyclub where we drank beer and ate pretzels until our delayed flight was finally called. Loni berated the training. She cynically called the course the latest fancy of our marketing department. "I have seen them come and seen them go. They are all about the same."

Loni has been in this job too long, I thought to myself.

On the flight home, I sat next to a man from Kenya. He was studying in Minneapolis and planned to return to Africa once he graduated. He was idealistic. He wanted to return home after his graduation to fix the "big problems" in his country. I told him that those big problems may never be solved. I advised that perhaps he should stay in the US, get a job, get married and enjoy life. From my TotalCom perspective at that time, trying to change the world wasn't worth the effort. Best to give up and be happy now. My seatmate wasn't going to be persuaded. He had a mission. I shrugged as the plane rolled down a solid white runway and disappeared into a cloud of snowflakes. The plane shook violently as we climbed through the storm. Above the cloud bank was that amazing sight I had seen so many winters in Minnesota. The stars were set like diamonds on the blackest sheet of night imaginable.

Monday morning back in Minnesota, I tried out the new techniques I learned in Milwaukee. I quizzed my sales team on how much they had prepared for their meetings that week. I am sure I sounded crazy, but I figured practice makes perfect. I signed up for Friday webinars to get refresher training in the Science of Selling methods. It helped to calm my nerves and gave me a new sense of purpose with my team. I figured if I could become the best at the new selling method, perhaps I could manage my way out of my nightmare.

Meanwhile, TotalCom commissioned a large management consulting company to assess what was broken with the sales force. Predictably, the ensuing report found that TotalCom's sales team was woefully behind the competition and the rest of the world in many respects. The report found that TotalCom sales teams were generally unable to articulate a clear 'value proposition' to customers. It seemed that no one could explain to our customers why they should buy from TotalCom as opposed to our competitors. This troubling news was not exactly a revelation to me. Just as muscles you don't use tend to atrophy, if you have a sales team that is bogged down servicing clients, it will never know how to pitch a value proposition and sell. A sales person's worth at TotalCom was tied to the ability to provide good customer service on existing products. New sales were awarded to TotalCom by customers based on service heroics by the sales teams and quid pro quos instead of an ability to truly differentiate the company from competition. Sales people were expected to stay up all night helping maintenance crews trouble shoot critical problems. And that is the way clients wanted it. It gave them control. If the sales team did not keep service running, the team would take a beating and certainly would not be given any new business. The sales teams became conditioned to never take an eye off customer service. The apocalypse had happened. The question from my initial TotalCom sales interview had been answered. Always service a customer's needs ahead of trying to make a sale. Regardless of what we did to offload non-sales work onto other job functions, the sales force could not truly become a sales force as long as the customers controlled the game. Furthermore, the sales team had largely forgotten how to sell. The 30 year paycheck is not about risking your job to get a large commission check. Commoditization of TotalCom's services was a reality because customers forced our sales teams to believe the products were commodities. This was the report the Big Eight consultancy gave us. It also explained why adoption of the Science of Selling program was not yielding the expected results. A new plan was needed. Each sales person would need to role play a sales opportunity in front of a panel that included management and outsiders to become certified at selling in the new and more aggressive manner.

Certifications always appear to be a re-interview for a job you are already doing. In some cases, people had been in the same titles for ten or even twenty years. Why did they need to certify for a job they had been doing so long? It was really too hard to explain the reason, let alone defend the premise. No one was happy about it. So, I just put down the gavel and told everyone it was an edict coming from upper management and we had to get it done.

There is no way to become more quickly seen as an inconsequential pawn than to give up on rationalizing decisions you don't own. By telling my team members they would have to follow orders with no reason why, I was admitting that I either did not have the power to push back, did not know or did not care. While the former was true, I actually thought this certification was needed. The team particularly hated the idea of the role plays and they resented that I would be the judge. They also asked why I did not have to be certified in my role. Truthfully, I would have loved to have done the certification. Any chance to truly sell even in a role play sounded like a picnic compared to my present job of pushing paper and defending myself from internal attack.

There is nothing more painful than listening to someone who is ill-prepared trying to figure out what the audience wants to hear during a role play performance. Thankfully, there were time limits on the role plays, but in some cases it appeared that the speaker had done the impossible and made time stop altogether. These sales people were great at troubleshooting a service outage, but relied on specialists and technical teams to give inspiring presentations. Now, with the methods of the Science of Selling thrown in, 30 year vets were reduced to stammering. The teams were wallowing in it. The presentations were equally frustrating to score. More of the team was failing than passing. It was my job to deliver pass or fail grades to each team member. The many who failed got the 'look on the bright side, at least you get to practice again' speech. This made me even less popular with the team and morale was hitting an all-time low. Little did I realize that the biggest loser in this certification game was me. Regardless of the fact that I had only been managing a majority of the team for four months, all eyes shifted to the leadership. How could so many people be failing? Rhonda most certainly was not going under on this one. It was about this time that she started talking with Loni about replacing me. Without even opening her mouth, Loni had manipulated Rhonda into the frame of mind she was trying to get Frank into a year ago. I needed to go. The team needed better management. I was not even respected by most of them. Rhonda no doubt agreed, if for no other reason than self-preservation.

Minneapolis Act III

Loni wanted me back in the sales ranks. She saw me as a sales widget, not fit for management at our illustrious firm. What I didn't realize at the time was that her accolades about my selling prowess were sincere. She thought I was a great sales person and would do just fine as a salesperson under her for the remainder of her career. Finding driven and hard-working sales people is not easy in an environment that favors the safety-conscious. I could have passed the certification in my sleep. At TotalCom, employees often fall into one of two traps. Either they play it too safe and lose their effectiveness or remain too ambitious and grow discontent with waiting and wondering why their good ideas are ignored time and again. The ambitious are rarely ready to wait ten years for a promotion.

An executive at TotalCom was the first to point this out to me. The time between promotions at TotalCom hardly keeps you incented to keep trying. Consider this. If you begin with the company right out of college you can expect at some point to be promoted to a second level job. There might even be a 10% increase in salary at that point. Getting to a third level will generally take on average an additional ten years. This can go more quickly if you are lucky or, in some cases, it may never happen. The third promotion comes only to a lucky few of the upwardly mobile. The rest of the pack may wait until the tail end of its career, or may never occur. This executive (who had seen three promotions) was about 25 years into his career. This made no sense if you wish to incent human beings to do their best day in and day out. A lot of studies have been done on 'gamification.' Gamification is the notion that employees stay more engaged and continue to strive if they are regularly rewarded. The system at TotalCom was anything but regular. But if the company would cut the promotions into three mid-level steps with 3% raises included along the way, it would be much easier to keep employees motivated. The mean time between a promotion would be cut from ten years to three without dramatically increasing the cost to the company. Instead, the Human Resources Vice President at TotalCom started distributing a four page document annually that outlines every fringe benefit and the related dollar value to an employee. If you count everything including my employee discounts and liberal use of the company bathrooms and heating and air-conditioning, I was making far more than I ever dreamed. Somehow it falls flat. It seems like a ploy to preach the poor man rich in order to keep contentment in the ranks.

While Loni and Rhonda plotted my demise and brainstormed a replacement, the summer months rolled in. In Minnesota, that meant that no one works on Friday and the cities are dead each weekend. Nearly everyone tries to escape to a north woods cabin to enjoy the brief, beautiful weather in a state known for the opposite. But I had taken two weeks in the spring to go to Spain with my family with commission monies I had saved, and was relegated to office duty for the long hot summer. The office seemed particularly lonesome on Fridays. Sales people are often out of the office on appointments, but this summer felt different. It felt like they were purposefully staying away. Could anyone blame them? I owned the entire seventh floor of the building. Some days I could shoot an arrow through the floor and not hit a soul. I sat deep in thought at the big oak desk I inherited from Tim, my former mentor. I didn't see any way out and I kept hoping and praying for something to happen. I needed a break, and it seemed like I always got one just as things looked their most bleak. It was in a moment like this that Frank had pulled me up from the medical device account disaster. I went through my shoebox of business cards. I took stock of my LinkedIn connections. I had been extremely picky about who I connected with over the years. I had less than a hundred professional connections. When I was kicking down my number as a hotshot salesman, that seemed like ten connections too many. Now it seemed like a hundred too few. I picked up the phone and called an old colleague. He was now working for a competitor. He told me they were hiring, but not in the management ranks. He knew a head hunter and promised to put me in touch.

I interviewed with smaller technology companies all summer. Each interview ended poorly as we shared a common distrust for each another. After seventeen years, I was definitely an TotalCom'er. The competitors felt I was just interviewing for the sake of interviewing or possibly to negotiate better pay at TotalCom. The competitor's hiring managers had hired TotalCom people for sure, but not before layoff season. Layoffs were still a few months out. 'What is he up to?', they thought.

Also, with the amount of experience and time, experience and success I had with TotalCom, these shrewd managers at the biggest competitors couldn't fathom that I was on the bubble. After all, objects at rest tend to stay at rest. The distrust manifested itself in several ways with my interviewers. Some chuckled and laughed and asked why I would be interested in leaving TotalCom. Others challenged me to explain why I was interviewing, before we even got started. The recruiters I worked with rolled their eyes. It would kill their reputations if I did not make myself first believable, and second actually take the job if offered. No second interviews came from four first interviews. I decided to hunker down and see what would happen. This year's layoff season was rumored to be a 'hair cut' with minimal disruptions for the first time in three years.

My last meeting for the year with Loni was scheduled just days before layoff day. She was more erratic than ever, suggesting that I should "take my under-performers out behind the shed (and chop off their heads)" and that so-and-so, "had no business being in the sales role he was in." So much for an even hand. I hardly blinked. What could I do? I wanly agreed and walked out of her office. I was a shadow of the guy who had met with Loni just nine months earlier, ready to take on the world with a promotion.

We followed the normal protocol on layoff day. Everyone was called into the office early and awaited a call from their supervisor to find out their status. Normally, I sat in with Frank during the proceedings, but Rhonda didn't ask for my help. Protocol also dictated managers went first and then the sales teams. I arrived early and waited for the call. My phone rang and I walked over to Rhonda's corner office. "You have been retained" is all she said. Good, I thought, safe again. Following my ritual I waited until the entire sales force got their news. I studied their reactions (which was never good no matter their status), and went out to lunch alone as soon as the crowd had filtered out to the bar. In the Skyway I walked in a daze. I noticed people getting on and off at elevator banks at the Oracle building and at the USBank building. I wondered what was going on in everyone else's world today. "We had our layoffs today", I felt like saying to a particularly dour woman who caught my eye. At lunch I thought about the future. Specifically, I thought about the next twelve months. What would I be doing next fall? It seemed utterly impossible that I would still be managing this team, but I had been retained. I guess that meant that the smart money was on me staying where I was.

The next Monday, Rhonda called me into her office.

"We're thinking about reassigning you." By 'we' she most certainly meant Loni. "Reassignment". This was a new one on me. Was I being let go? I couldn't be. Otherwise, they would have just told me that the week before. "Great!" I said, trying to smile. "What is the new assignment?" Rhonda looked down at her desk. She was obviously now mimicking Loni's clean desk policy. "We're not sure..." she said with a concerned look.

She didn't know? How can you reassign someone without knowing where you were going to put them? I couldn't get beyond my blinders. Obviously, Loni wanted me out and it wasn't as though I was going to get a promotion out of the deal. But what did she want me to do? I asked Rhonda what I should do next. She asked me to keep it quiet. "Should I begin looking for a job?"

"Yeah", she said, "and let me know if I can help."

I walked out and immediately called Frank. We met near his downtown apartment. It wasn't pretty. I kept asking Frank what was going on and he kept telling me I was done in the manager role. Loni was throwing her weight around and pulling me off the field. I couldn't accept it. I hadn't lost my job, but my dignity had been stripped. Frank said it wasn't likely that I would be traded to a new team and that could only mean one thing. Loni wasn't done with me. She must have something in mind for me on her team. But if she did, why didn't she just come out and tell me? What I couldn't anticipate was she wanted me to trade places with someone on the team. That person was Mickey.

Frank promised to help. He said he would put out the word and ask his boss about any openings. "Manager openings?" I asked. He nodded his head and looked away. The next few weeks were the beginning of a mad dash to talk to everyone I knew about openings inside of Total-Com. I called upon acquaintances from Brussels to California. I was determined to make this my exit from Minneapolis. I motivated myself by imagining that I would be let go if I didn't find something. I told my family that we had to be ready to move. My wife and I furiously began to paint the kitchen. A management job opened in Nashville. I talked with the hiring manager. I knew the guy and had positive interactions with him in the past. He was high on my prospects. I told him I could be in Tennessee by January first. But then he went dark. Eventually, he returned my emails saying that he was going another direction with the hire. It felt like a cloud hung over my head. Everyplace I sensed an opening suddenly closed.

When I mentioned this to Frank, he suggested I go see Loni one more time. Loni accepted the meeting and when asked about the 'reassignment', she assured me that there would be a job for me. I asked her how long I had to find something. She said she thought it was only fair that

Minneapolis Act III

I find a new job by January first. I asked for her to write a reference to a couple of internal jobs for which I was a long shot. She complied without letting me see the emails she had written.

Behind the scenes Frank had found an opening for me. It was a same level job, but not in management. It was in small markets, supporting sales teams in Illinois, Iowa and Nebraska. It was a technical specialist job, so I would not be directly selling. I would just consult with sales people and customers on our complex products. Due to my time with the medical device account, I knew the products better than most, so the team was excited about having me come on board. The dark clouds had temporarily parted, but I wasn't really and truly so excited. Frank reasoned with me. Did I want to face the humiliation of having to trade places with Mickey? With this new job, I could collect at least a few ounces of dignity and walk away. Frank explained that a management job could open on the small markets team and I could get back to my old managerial level. My mind was racing. Too much was happening too quickly. I needed to find a safe place before the holidays. It was already the second week in December.

Frank was right. The next day would be our last weekly Loni meeting of the year. I needed to get this settled. I applied for the job on-line and set up a call with the hiring manager. The last thing I needed to do was to tell Loni. Without her consent, I would not be allowed to take the new job. She wanted me out, so I assumed it would just be a formality. I gave her the news after our weekly call. Rhonda looked on dumbfounded. Both of them were unaware. Loni asked me where I was in the process and what the vice president in the small markets group had to say?

I told her I had applied for the job and that the vice president was on board. Loni looked furious. I have never seen her so mad. She thought for a moment. Her face went several shades of red. She didn't want to keep me, and she didn't want to let me go. Her expression belied her confusion. She thought silently for what seemed like an eternity. She finally said, "Ok, I will agree to that." I didn't realize how badly I had messed up her plans. She wanted me to take Mickey's job, but she didn't yet have the pieces in place with human resources. I will never understand why she told me about the 'reassignment' when she did. She could have waited and trapped me with the element of surprise. But in telling me about the reassignment before she had her plans complete, she saved me from having to admit my failure to a team of people who hated me already. I had slipped out of her grasp. I was free, yet drifting off to unknown lands in a very tattered vessel. I took the last two weeks of the month off and drove east to see my parents for Christmas. Ho, ho, ho. The sun set over the Ohio cornfields and the radio blared Johnny Cash. "That old wheel is going to roll around again/ and when it does/it will even up the score…" I had been beaten. But I was still employed. Cash kept belting it out. I intended to even up this score. I promised myself that I would not be in this job any longer come next December. I was going to take a different approach. Being 'safe' was not going to be good enough. The next year was going to require more offense than defense.

This is where things get good. Our protagonist (me) has been thoroughly chased up a tree and the trunks have been set afire with gasoline. My enemies have built a trench around the tree and filled the make-shift moat with molten lava. The only thing that can save me is a friendly and extremely oversized bird or a helicopter.

I really had to choose between two things. I could slip into anonymity and ride out, to whatever extent possible, my 30 year paycheck not knowing when the last installment would come. Or I could start making some major changes in how I had been playing this game. The biggest motivator for me was that I had been totally humiliated, pushed into a corner and told to sit. I was a sorry looking dog on a very short leash. When we first met, one of the directors for the new team I supported asked me, "What happened to you?" with the look of smelling a rotten egg. It was hard for me to explain.

So, I spent some time figuring out exactly what had happened to me with the intention of not letting it happen again. I also needed to be able to articulate it to anyone I met so that they understood who they were dealing with and what they might and might not expect of me.

I slowly realized two things.

First, I stopped being me right after the reorganization brought me back into Loni's fold. I tried to be Loni instead, hoping she would have mercy on me. But by trying to be someone else I became utterly invisible. I became nothing. This is why there are so many in the ranks inside large corporations who don't seem to exist. They run their meetings, reviews and their business in a manner they think will be pleasing to others. They act in a manner that mirrors what they are subjected to by their superiors. They become cheap copies of other cheap copies. No wonder innovation suffers. So, if Loni is going to have weekly reviews where she goes around the room asking each Sales Center vice president to talk about the week's sales results, I should do the same with my team. Without fitting in, how can we expect to be liked, let alone promoted? The problem is that, by disengaging from what makes us what we are, we become invisible to everyone around us. Each initiative looks like the last with a tired cadence of meetings and reviews. Tactics and strategies becomes robotic. Rolling out training isn't about philosophically discussing and changing how we might engage with customers. Instead it is a spreadsheet of on-line course completions, rote memorization and testing. Red-yellow-green reports for middle managers track the milestone completions and determine their efficacy to the firm. Where is the success story that tracks a change in behavior to a positive customer interaction or, God forbid, a sale? One thousand swinging hammers manage many of the biggest businesses in America. New ideas come from outside and are assimilated by those hammers into the day to day work. Any creativity growing in the ranks is piteously beaten into submission. I decided with this new job I was going to start doing things my way. I was going to start making my best judgment of what should be done in any situation and let that be my ultimate guide. Come what may, even if my 30 year paycheck ended early.

The second thing I realized was that I needed other people. I had spent far too long trying to do everything myself. Other's losses were not my wins. I decided life is not a zero-sum game. Not unless I had done everything I could to help my peers was I doing my best. This included consoling them during hard times. Up until now, I had stayed employed and I was on track for retirement and having funds to send our kids to college. But, so what? I had isolated myself so that I could stay on the payroll. As Charles Dicken's Jacob Marley chides his counting house partner Scrooge: "Mankind was my business...!"

I needed more than just a future. I needed a future where I stood a chance of something truly good happening to me. I made a goal that I would add a hundred quality connections to my LinkedIn page each year. I would also reach out and connect with twenty of my contacts each month for no other reason than to see how they were doing. It was a difficult goal. But I needed to make my network relevant to my trajectory. I needed positive people by my side. I began thinking of my network as the people who would help me along my long journey to the place I chose to march. And because I planned on marching to a very scary place, I needed a legion of the best and most supportive people I could find. Furthermore, I needed to help others. I pledged to introduce people in my network to people who could help them. Whether it was introducing a colleague unhappy in her job to people I knew in other departments or companies who were looking to hire, or helping another sales person from a different industry get connected to my customer, I was going to model collaboration. I would ask for nothing in return. As I brought this plan into action I often told people I had helped to "Pay it forward."

Now that I understood what had happened to me and how to avoid it, I had one last thing to do. I needed to figure out what I wanted. The manager deflection technique of asking the employee who is bored or sick of a current job, "Well, what do you want to do?" just to shut him up needed to be turned into my weapon. I actually did need to figure out what I wanted to do and start marching in that direction. I also needed to keep marching and not give up or get distracted. I needed to accept that times may get difficult, but I would not compare myself to others or stop when I found myself making less money or on the brink. I wracked my brain and all I knew was I wanted to be noticed for something I did. Working on small accounts as a subject matter specialist was never going to get me there. I needed to be in control of whatever it was I would be doing so I could make a name for myself and it needed to be big. I needed to get reconnected with larger accounts to create my big success and catapult to a better place.

As it stood, I was working with some of the smallest accounts our division supported. The job was easy and I was welcomed with open arms into the new group. By following through with my promise to use my creativity and best judgment, I inadvertently became extremely popular with the sales teams I supported. I began to negotiate price directly with customers over the phone. The TotalCom process is for sales teams to work with pricing teams and their management to get custom discounts. The pricing teams were a cantankerous lot. Not only were they slow, they rarely gave the prices asked for on the first request. This chewed up time and gave TotalCom a reputation of being inflexible and slow in addressing customer needs. More than once I had seen a customer go with competitor because he could not wait for the pricing decisions. The worst thing for any sales person was to lose a deal while having the winning price in her hand two days too late. I had been around so long I knew the approximate discounts the pricing personnel would eventually agree to, so I just priced a little higher than that and gave quotations on the phone. We would often negotiate deals without our finance teams ever being involved. Once a price was agreed to, then, and only then, would we go to the pricing group. We let the client know we needed a few weeks to work the 'internal process' to get the contract, leaving time for the inevitable slog with the pricing team. The advantage was that we knew exactly what was needed to get the contract from the customer and there was never a second request to the crusty pricing team because the price had already been agreed to with the client.

This way of doing things is absolute heresy inside a command-and-control culture that sees the cycles and process as a mini version of the checks and balances in our government. From my point of view, we were not a government, but more like a Boy Scout troop trying to find our way out of the woods.

The sales teams insisted I help them in the field. I was their lucky horseshoe and my approach was creating a lot of wins. I made a point of not skimping on the travel budget. If my presence was valuable, it cost money to the firm. If it wasn't, I would stay home. Many in the corporate culture get shamed into traveling like a peasant throughout all of Christendom to try to fit into the corporate budget. Meanwhile, armies of executives crisscross the blue sky on-board private jets. I am not advocating that we all take a private jet, but I am saying if we are going to travel we need to have the self-esteem to spend what it takes to travel comfortably AND bring our A-game into our day's work. Otherwise, stay at home. For me that meant visiting five clients a day, including breakfast, lunch and dinner meetings and kicking back at a decent hotel when the day was done. The numbers skyrocketed and I got a warning on my mid-year review for breaking the bank in expenses.

I was working my new job from home, and when I wasn't on the road, I was listening to endless conference calls from the comfort of my home office. On our team calls, I made a point of cleaning the bathroom each week. I would fold clothes or do other chores during other internal calls. I always brought what I had to the customer engagements. As a result, I was constantly late or behind on my internal metrics. I completely ignored them and concentrated on selling things. I wanted to prove to myself that I still had the right stuff.

I pioneered the use of LinkedIn to get to know our customers in advance of sales calls and I even correlated different customers in the same geographical area in order to suggest joint discussions and sales campaigns. Money was coming in hand over fist. My commission checks were fat and my home expenses were minimal. I wore tee-shirts and jeans when I wasn't traveling, and the car rarely left the garage. Still, it was not a siren's song for me. I was beginning to intuit that the 30 year paycheck was not a goal in and of itself. I spent each day being me, but I had my bags packed for the journey I was ready to take.

On Friday afternoons, I combed through company organization charts and my LinkedIn contacts looking for a way out of my present job so I could begin making my long march to my eventual goal. Again, all I knew at the time was if I got attached to a large account and was myself, the right things would happen. One day in late spring, I noticed in a company newsletter a story of a big sale that happened in the southeast. Thompson was the sales center vice president. He had supported my sales region years ago. I reached out and congratulated him on the win. He wrote right back and asked what I was up to. I told him, and added that I was in search of new opportunities. He wanted me to talk to one of his directors about an Account Manager position. The title was the same as the one I had ten years ago when I last talked to Thompson. Like Loni, he saw me as a great whatever-it-was-I-was-at-the-time-he-first-met-me. There was nothing I could do about that. My goal was to get on a large account, and Thompson had one for me.

Chapter 12

My March on Atlanta

Jessica, Thompson's director, called me the next week. Blue Star in Atlanta was a stagnant account. After the merger, TotalCom stopped using them as a vendor, and our business and executive relationships fell by the wayside. Jessica was being pressured to either fix the situation or have it fixed for her. In case you haven't been paying attention for the past one hundred plus pages, that meant she needed to either fire her existing account manager or face being fired herself. During the phone interview, she was as tough as she could be on me about my experience and capabilities. But after the hour was up, I felt she had warmed to the real me and not any propped-up version. Of course, it was always hard to tell if you were talking to the actual person or some version of their boss whom they were parroting. Jessica asked me to put a PowerPoint together on how I would handle Bluestar, and send it down to her.

Fair enough. Besides our balance of trade problem, the IT team saw us a supplier and not a partner. Our existing business with them was substantial and each year the IT department tried to decrease it in order to make their bonuses by cutting costs. New projects being sponsored by the business units at Bluestar were flatly going to other vendors. IT liked punishing us and wanted to keep us in our place. In my Power-Point deck, I suggested we take a new approach. I had seen this situation before, and had beaten the system by creating relationships with the budget holders. Never mind that this had also gotten me removed from the account. If we needed change, this approach would certainly bring change. But how were we going to create these relationships? If we did not know the buyers, how would we get their attention? I started thinking about LinkedIn. I spent the next few days researching people on LinkedIn from Bluestar. I decided to include a social media focus into my PowerPoint to Jessica. This approach most likely seemed very odd, but I got the job. It meant we would need to move to Atlanta.

Nobody in my house wanted to move. This was just the first hurdle I would face. I convinced my family that the 30 year paycheck was a lie. It could end at any time. More importantly, I needed this change. I couldn't stay in Minneapolis and effectively make the career journey I needed to make. For one, I knew too many people in the Minnesota branch. I had done almost every job in every sales segment. Minneapolis is a not a huge market and people tended to stay in their positions in order to collect the 30 year paycheck. Moving to another telecom company also posed a danger for me. The market is small in Minneapolis and everyone knew me and my reputation. It felt like too much baggage. I needed to get into a market where I was new and where I could experiment without worrying about what had happened to me or who was whispering about it behind my back. This may seem like a really stupid reason to move your family one thousand miles south after seventeen years of creating deep friendships and community ties. You are probably right. Yet it is what I needed to do to break the cycle.

Block by block I began knocking down the fortress of protection I had built around me. I painted over the weathered notches on the kitchen wall that indicated how tall my children were at each birthday. I took conference calls in my car while the real estate agent showed our house. We cleaned the bathrooms daily—always ready for showings. We began emptying out the attic. I threw away the lawn signs I had accumulated for St Paul candidates and protesting the first war in Iraq. We spent our evenings on the Internet looking at property in Atlanta. Because the new job was not a promotion, TotalCom did not want to change my salary or provide any moving assistance. My entitlement bubbled up. How dare they! But this was my move and I needed to own it. I needed to push myself out of complacency and dependency. My wife and I had put together a cash emergency fund of eight months of salary in case I got laid off. We spent every dime selling our house, buying a new one in Atlanta and paying the moving expenses.

At the last minute Nicole, the Regional Vice President in Atlanta got cold feet on the deal and would not sign the offer letter. Normally, this would send me into a tailspin. It signaled danger in the transition. It also signaled that Nicole was unsure of me. There were so many negative vibes I couldn't count them. On that same day, we accepted an offer on our St Paul home. I took vacation days and flew to Atlanta. Our good friends Rex and Ursula put me up for the week as I house hunted for the cheapest decent house I could find. I made an offer on a house that Friday and flew home to an early November snow storm. We gave away furniture and took truckloads of stuff to Goodwill. Nicole finally signed the offer letter and I accepted. I vowed that I would not stay in the job more than eighteen months. I was on a mission. I was going to shake things up. TotalCom would not save me or preserve my life or lifestyle.

THE 30 YEAR PAYCHECK

I had me and my network. I possessed no celebrity status because I got a check every two weeks from TotalCom. The last thing I did before I left St Paul was to throw my parka in a garbage bag bound for recycling. As I did so, I saw the tips of my scuffed cordovan shoes sticking up. My wife had jettisoned them as part of the move. They were supposed to last me a lifetime according to the salesman. I could not wear them any longer because the leather was destroyed from misuse, but I refused to get rid of them. I thought about pulling them out of the bag. Something stopped me. In my shirt sleeves I quickly got into my blue Subaru by myself and left. I was bound for Atlanta where I would meet the moving van and unpack. My family would drive separately and meet me the day before Christmas.

As I drove, I thought only briefly about the going-away parties and all our good friends in St Paul. I want to be clear. I love them all dearly and they have been an important part of my life and the life of my family. But I needed to push it all away. I needed to break the cycle of the 30 year paycheck. The only way I could do that was to live freely and let the road be my guide. Cruising through Iowa, I logged into my conference calls for my old job and didn't even listen. There. I had checked a box. I stopped in Iowa City for lunch. I arrived in St Louis and stayed with a college friend. I arrived around 5 pm. His son is a good piano player. My friend explained when I got there that his son was learning to play the organ at church and we would pick him up and then head out for dinner. It started to rain as we got out of his car in the church parking lot. We silently entered the empty church. The organ was softly playing a carol for the coming Christmas Eve service. My friend's son was barely reaching the pedals and his teacher looked on critically. We slipped into a pew and I looked up at the stained glass windows. They were gray and dull in the coming night. The sulfur lamps in the parking lot illuminated the rain that streaked the glass vertically like tears.

I asked myself in the silence if this move was the right thing to do. The answer I got back was this: A pair of fourteen year old feet stretching for the pedals with maximum effort. Silent Night was shaping up. I wondered what I was teaching my kids right now. My daughter was certainly bawling her eyes out about leaving her friends. We would spend the holidays alone in a new city and in a new house. Nothing was going to be the same. But, in truth, nothing had changed. This was the same earth, the same people. Without trying to be more, we will never know what we are made of. What would fifteen more years of steady paychecks bring us in St Paul? It might be just fine and comfortable. But my question remained: what was I made of? I would never know without trying. This was my way of beginning to break away. I was beginning to see that nothing was tethering me to my old existence. No amount of time spent in corporate America meant that I was owed anything. I was the sum of my talents and risks I would take. If I chose to exercise neither, I certainly could expect nothing more than whatever was around each corner. What is more frightening? Going downhill on a bike blindfolded or pumping the pedals. Either way could be a disaster. Either way I could fail. But I wanted to own my destiny no matter what it was.

The next day I left St Louis before dawn while everyone was still asleep and crossed the Mississippi for the last time. For years I ran every other day over that river in St Paul on my route that took me across two different bridges. The river was much wider in St Louis. It churned a black muddy color from high above on the bridge I now crossed. By lunch time, I was in Nashville and I arrived at the Decatur, Georgia post office at 4:55 pm to pick up my mail. I approached our new house in the driving rain. The storm drains were clogged from months of lack of maintenance. I didn't care. I unlocked the front door and surveyed the sea of boxes the movers had unloaded. I felt at ease and I decided that this was just the beginning. Tomorrow I would go to the office and begin a new chapter. I was given the chance to try one more time. I knew that night that what I was planning to do would most certainly be misunderstood and probably catapult me out of my new safe haven job and onto the streets. I was at peace with that, though. It would be a grand success or failure. Either way, it would be misunderstood by the 30 year paycheck gang. But this time, nothing was going to stop me from doing it my way.

No one was in the office. After all, it was two days before Christmas. Vacation time is allotted by the number of years of service one has, and in a company where everyone tends to stay for a long time, massive vacation burn-off happens over the holidays. It seems this is the only acceptable time not to work. The main reason is that no one else is working either. You can't be faulted for taking these weeks off the same way you can't be faulted for not coming into the office on a Saturday. Two weeks before the end of the year, email missives are sent by mid and upper management telling everyone to 'recharge your batteries' for the new year. This is followed by a big hearty thanks for all the long hours and hard work. Everyone goes home and tries to forget they work at a place where they need two weeks to recharge their batteries at the end of each year just to be able to drag their carcass into the office for the next fifty weeks.

I need no recharging this year. Like Scrooge's clerk Mr. Cratchit, I sat with a single light in an otherwise darkened twelfth floor, putting together a PowerPoint deck that would serve as my mantra for changing direction with my new customer, and changing my life in the process. The desk I was assigned was dusty and full of old computer monitors. No one really cared that I was there. Instead of being insulted, it validated my energies as I worked. Bluestar, as I mentioned, had fallen out of favor with TotalCom, and the technology department wanted to make sure it was clear how inconsequential TotalCom really was. Even when lunch was included in the invitation, my emails and phone calls asking Bluestar to meet and talk were ignored. This wasn't a surprise to me. I knew I had to try the traditional routes as a formality, and I knew my efforts would fail. The difference was, at Bluestar these emails were perfunctory only. I had another plan of attack altogether. I was going on the offensive just as soon as the new year rolled around.

As I began to type at my solitary desk, I felt a shadow fall over my sordid computer-monitor filled space. "Hello?" said a female southern accent. I looked around and there stood Amanda. I hadn't seen her in fifteen years. She had trailed her husband to Minneapolis and worked on the same sales team with the Hedgehog. I had no idea she had moved back south, let alone that she was still with the company. She quizzed me on my career. I began to feel embarrassed. I had been knocked down a notch and it was easy to visualize my presence in Atlanta as a man on the run with his tail between his legs. I tried to keep my story factual and to the point. Amanda spun a fine tale of her whereabouts which included having children and now working in the same job I had but on a different account. I smiled. I wasn't sure of much, but I knew talking with her was not helping me get where I was going. In my nineteen months with the Atlanta team, I spoke to her only one other time. I was at the point of quitting when she called me out of the blue. I am not sure if she wanted to get the scoop or what, but I kept that conversation short. I am not trying to sound like a snob. In fact, it is my own failing that made me treat her this way. I needed to stay away from my past. I needed to be free of the way things were done in the Atlanta office. I knew that conceptually it was no different than the Minneapolis branch. I was not strong enough to stick to my new mission and, at the same time, gossip and rumor and share other small talk with Amanda. I was here to smash all the old mentality and grind up the shards. I needed space to do it.

My family arrived that night. I was drinking a beer alone and trying to get a television signal on the TV I had just pulled from a moving box. As they pulled in the driveway around mid-night the rain stopped. They were going on adrenaline. They loved the new house-- what they could see of it in the dark. The next day, I took them by the Elementary School where the kids would soon be going to school. A soaking rain had started again. My daughter cried. My son ran around the muddy playground. We got a pizza. Happy New Year! The next day the kids went to school and I went back to work on that PowerPoint.

My March on Atlanta

In the presentation, I laid out my tenets for the coming sales year:

1. The technology group wouldn't help TotalCom with getting new projects.
2. Nonetheless, new projects would be funded at Bluestar.

Therefore:

1. I would not worry about the technology group.
2. I would focus on creating new relationships with the business units.

This may not sound very profound. It may even appear to be common sense. But for a sales force that had been selling to technologists for the past seventy years, it was unique. However, no matter how revolutionary this may have seemed, no one would really care what the account manager planned to do. It was assumed that the compensation plan and management directives would drive behavior anyway. In other words, the reaction to my plan was, "That's nice. Sounds good. Now get to work and create some results." I had written the plan for me and no one else. I needed to create a compass point that I would follow and a mode of operation that made sense. This PowerPoint sat on my desk guiding me for the next eighteen months. As an example, when no one from the technology team attended the first six months of operational meetings, I sent a note asking them to tell me what they wanted to see for the next year because the meetings weren't well attended the year before. When I got no response to that request, I assumed they did not care if we met at all, and I freed up one more hour each month to pursue my plans. I used their silence to give me an advantage.

I knew that with equal or greater fervor I needed to create new relationships inside the business units at Bluestar. Otherwise, I would have nothing to show from this new approach. This was going to be tricky because there was no one to introduce me to them and my experience has been that no one at Bluestar responded to emails requesting meetings from outside vendors. I got lucky the first month, though. I snared a meeting with a senior business leader who gave me thirty minutes that taught me a lot. She was intrigued by my approach of offering her a business solution using technology. The problem was that as much as vendors wanted to meet with her, they spoke a language only the technology team understood. She was afraid that if she made the wrong move, the technology team would make her pay for not getting them involved. In other words, Bluestar business units needed good, non-technical advice that would keep them out of the cross-hairs of their technology department and would enable them to offer innovative solutions on time and on budget to grow the business.

Business leaders need to hear new ideas and have a vendor who can cover all the details from start to finish. This became my mantra for the blogs I would later write. I always thought of this one customer when I sat and created a new blog post. Keep it simple, keep it insightful, and cover all the details with whatever technology solution you propose. The more the solutions seemed to be all inclusive, the less fear the business units had that they would make the wrong decision and need to be bailed out by their technology team.

Another end of year task was to meet with the outgoing sales person. The guy whose job I was taking had been run out by Jessica before she was deemed to be the problem and moved onto a mid-market team. It really wasn't his fault that things were going poorly with Bluestar. If anything, he was doing what he was told. He had gotten a Bluestar badge so he could spend a lot of time with them. If Bluestar needed service help, he was called on. They even told Jessica that "He takes a good beating". While Jessica wanted more from him, he was doing exactly what he was tacitly asked to do: take a beating. He talked with me for almost an hour about who to avoid, what various Bluestar employees were like and, in fact, all his history with them. Yawn. I listened, smiled and took very few notes. My plan didn't include most of the people he had on his list. In one of those strange chance occurrences, my wife ran into him a few months later. It turned out that his son and my daughter took guitar lessons from the same instructor in Decatur. My wife noticed the TotalCom emblem on his iPad and asked if he worked there. He replied, "Sadly enough, I do." My wife then told him that I worked there too in business sales. He said he was sorry to hear that and proceeded to knock TotalCom every way he could. My wife couldn't believe it. It begs the question why anyone remains with a company they feel is so dysfunctional. Think about it. This salesman was picking up his son at 4:30 in the afternoon. Shouldn't he have been at work? I think that one reason people stick with the firm is because the company is so big and dysfunctional. It doesn't really matter what any one individual does. They are not only entitled to say bad things about it in public, but also can take liberties as they wish. Bashing TotalCom and leaving early is an entitlement for all the damaging ways the organization treats employees. So, making fun of TotalCom is not only something you can get away with, it is a privilege owed to you to equal out the abuse. This is utter insanity. TotalCom has no feelings or plans. TotalCom is nothing more than an idea put down on paper more than a century ago and stewarded along each day by thousands of souls who are trying to make the business profitable for their own betterment. There is nothing to get mad about unless you really care to look in the mirror and ask yourself why you continue to participate in the craziness. I had done just that the year before. I stopped participating and I was on my own trajectory. My intention was to lead, and if no one followed, I would walk out the door.

True to the aforementioned two-faced goddess Janus, January is always packed with finishing the work of the prior year and gearing up for the year ahead. The earliest I could get the entire extended team together to discuss Bluestar was the second week of the month. I scheduled two hours and invited all the technical and product specialists who had anything to do with Bluestar. My stated goals. First, I wanted ten solutions that we could sell Bluestar business leaders. The solutions had to make sense for Bluestar's vertical market and current financial and competitive environment. I wanted game-changing technology.

Second, for each of the ten solutions, I wanted to map them to business leaders at Bluestar who would benefit by them. This meant that each solution that benefited Bluestar's marketing endeavors should be tied to the Chief Marketing Officer or her staff. In some cases, we knew the names of the people we wanted to sell these solutions to, but in other cases we did not. For them, I just described the type of person who would want to know about the solution. For example: Human Resources Vice President.

I gave the plan to Jessica. She was impressed, but took a different type of plan to our sales leadership for approval. She presented a plan much like the one from the previous year. The plan that got the previous salesman removed. It was a plan filled with charts and graphs about current revenue trends and a smattering of big-bet sales that hadn't been socialized with anyone controlling a budget at Bluestar. Often you hear people say, "'hope' is not a sales strategy." I know why they say that. If we worked the plan Jessica submitted, we would have had nothing except hope for the year ahead.

But I marched forward with the plan I had submitted. My next step was to find as much information around the ten solutions as I could. There was plenty of technical information to read. The problem was there was nothing written about how the TotalCom products could come together to form a solution to improve customer services or help Bluestar's customers spend more money with Bluestar.

I had an idea on how to bridge this gap. The digital marketing manager for our sales division was located in Atlanta. I looked her up in late January for coffee. She owned our social media marketing efforts. I told her about my problem. I needed specific content that would lend credibility to the solutions I wanted to pitch to Bluestar. She suggested that if I could not find it, I should write it myself. She was looking for new bloggers to write about TotalCom solutions.

I have always enjoyed writing and I jumped at this opportunity. I had never blogged so I had a lot to learn. First, I needed to keep the posts short. Creating five-hundred words of impactful writing was like fitting together a jigsaw puzzle with extra pieces that ultimately needed to be tossed away. I needed to walk a fine line with my content. It needed to grab the attention of my target audience. Titles like "5 Ways Customer Service Is Changing Due To Mobile Applications", needed to be changed to "Top Trends In Mobile Marketing" to grab the attention of my marketing targets at Bluestar. By mentioning their vertical in the headline, I could tighten the connection even further. The content itself needed to be approachable and filled with stories and examples. I wanted to also make it easy to skim through. I used short sentences and left out complex structure so that the content stood out. I left out any technical jargon too. This would only scare the business leader off. I tried to make my arguments and examples simple so that they could be shared with anyone in the office and be readily understood. This took quite a bit of trial and error on my part, but I wasn't in it alone.

Corporate blogging wasn't well understood when the marketing manager first asked for the budget to start the program. Her vision was that she would get content from employees and post as regularly as possible. She struck a deal with a digital marketing firm in Atlanta to manage and edit the posts and got the green light. This created a petri dish for exploration on how to use the blog inside the business. Product teams were posting to get better awareness in the market about new products. Leaders were posting to provide thought leadership to the industry analysts. I was posting for all of the above with a specific twist. I wanted Bluestar to notice us and consider us an authority on the solutions they needed and we could supply. I wanted them to believe we had something they could not build themselves or get elsewhere. I reasoned that by making my content approachable to the business leaders, I could catch their attention first. That way they would ask for us to be included in their new plans. This would circumvent the technology team who would rather leave us off the list. I was given the guidelines to work with and the marketing team encouraged me to try out as many new ideas as I wanted. Eventually, I asked for images to be added to my blog posts, lending another dimension for engagement. I even played around with using video. I started with my ancient Canon Powershot propped on a step ladder in my living room. It worked fine. The videos had an amateur finish and made up for the veneer in genuineness.

Now all I needed was to get my target customers to look at my work. I knew the route would be social media, but I did not know the formula. At first, I tried to connect via LinkedIn, Twitter, etc with the people from Bluestar who fit the profile. This caused me heartache and em-barrassment as I learned by trial and error the perils of overstepping social norms in new media. Just like asking a business leader at his son's soccer game if he wanted to chat about your new idea, my direct tactics went over like a lead balloon. With the help of others online and the folks at our blog, I adapted my approach. I realized I needed to exist along-side my clients and not in their face. The best way to do this was to find the places my target market inhabited online and go there myself. I correlated LinkedIn Groups and Twitter followings by brute force. My eyes were often bleary by the end of the day. The scratch paper on my desk was filled with Twitter handles and names I had researched. I was looking for the holy grail of social media: influencers. I figured in order to be an influencer, I needed to interact with other influencers.

It was about this time I realized the importance of my own on-line persona. Not only did I need to tighten up my profile to exude the confidence of a thought-leader, but I needed to have some table stakes: a decent head shot photo, credentials and followers. I had a small but growing number of followers on LinkedIn and Twitter. I began to devote some of my day to interacting with interesting people in order to not only build my network, but to fill it with smart people. I looked for powerful connections and tried to interact with my whole network in a genuine way. I met many interesting people in Social Media from all over the country and began collaborating with them via comments on social media. This group of insiders would eventually convince me to begin my own business and helped me immensely with kind words and referrals at the start. I enlisted my best friend from high school to fly down to Atlanta and take my head shot photos.

This was the first significant spending I had done in my entire career. I had always waited for my company to invest in me and felt hurt when it didn't. What I failed to realize is that investing in myself was a much better deal. Yes, it required my own money, but I could decide how and what to invest. I could envision the purpose of investment and cash in as much as possible. By calling the shots myself, I could never be disappointed by lack of budget or follow through.

My days were consumed with writing comments on a myriad of online groups and responding to individuals who seemingly had nothing to do with Bluestar. I turned off my email feed for several hours a day to see how the comments ebbed and flowed. It enabled me to provide quick responses on comments to the content I had posted. I also spent hours honing my Twitter feeds to better pick up on news that I could share and write about. I took screen shots of my crowning achievements which included getting a business executive to follow me on Twitter and receiving a comment or 'like' from someone I had never heard of from an operations group at Bluestar. I continued to churn out new content each week. The days I published were the busiest for me. I pushed the content via many groups and several methods on Twitter. I spent the day creating snappy headlines to gain attention from readers. It was very different from my days as a salesperson in Minnesota. I sometimes wondered what I was doing. But small encouragement kept me going and ultimately, I succeeded.

Success did not come in the form of a white flag of surrender from Bluestar's cranky technology department or a big smooch from the business units. Instead, it came in like a lamb. That spring and summer we received six formal requests for proposal (RFP's). The previous eight months I had been attached to the account, we had gotten one. And that one RFP was for business we already had that presumably Bluestar wanted to give to another vendor. The RFP's we got were fascinating. Each one correlated back to one of the solutions from my plan that I blogged about. Each one pointed to a solution we had outlined during our planning session. Even more amazing were some of the questions in the RFP. Along with the normal questions, there were questions about how the technology could be used for future applications that transcended the utility of the products and services they wanted us to bid on. Many of the applications asked about were mentioned in my blog posts. Essentially, they were coming to us for advice. Furthermore, we were predisposed to win because we had already done our homework on the application side. We offered more than our competitors because we knew what the RFP authors wanted. They wanted to stick with a leader and they had begun to see us as that leader.

It is almost a letdown to say that we won two large bids from Bluestar worth almost $50 million in new revenue to TotalCom. When we asked our contact on the procurement team who had sponsored us to get on the RFP distribution list, she told us the business units wanted us included. She even admitted that the technology team was against adding us to the bidders, but had been over-ruled by the business units. While this wasn't helping our reputation with the technology team, we had earned TotalCom a nice boost.

After the accolades, money and award trips, I felt empty inside. I had placed all my energy into this new campaign and no one seemed to understand how important it was to the sale. They believed what I had done had worked, but no one was ready to drop their golf sticks and spend their day behind a screen on LinkedIn and Twitter to make the next big sale. With the sponsorship of my sales division, I began to give training discussions with TotalCom teams on the big success. The other sales teams loved the idea of making a lot of money and thought the approach was novel, but none of them took up the sword. The main objections I got were, "How am I going to find time to do this?" Every time I suggested carving out some time to work on it a little, it was met by fierce resistance and a litany of reasons it wouldn't happen.

My March on Atlanta

Ironically, the other road block for the sellers was that they were afraid of saying the wrong thing. It was ironic because there was so little editing and legal scrutiny on the blog back then. I assured them that they would not mess it up, but it was a real concern. After multiple trainings of several different levels and job titles, my idea was not taking off organically. The more I pushed and modeled the approach, the more interest I got from sales and marketing teams. I gave my pitch over and over again on how to include social selling in our plans, but I just could not get the idea to fully take flight.

I took stock of what I was doing. I was spending so much time pushing my idea that my eyes were firmly off of the ball with Bluestar. I was coasting on my big deals. In fits and starts I tried to rekindle my energy with Bluestar, but I just could not get my mind off of social selling. If I had earned TotalCom $50 million with it, why wasn't everyone all over me to replicate the success? Why wasn't I a hero?

Heroes at TotalCom are few and far between. Usually they are CEO's or top executives who find a way to maintain a sense of genuineness with their teams while continuing to make no sudden moves to derail their career. One such man was our executive sales vice president Curtis who I mentioned a few chapters back. As I said then, he was a large man who had been in the Marines prior to joining TotalCom. Curtis was unique in that he spent more time visiting the sales ranks than anyone in his job before or since. When he came out to Minneapolis to help me close the medical device deal, he put fear into vice president Loni's heart. Curtis wanted to know what was going on with the rank and file sellers, not a report from Loni telling him that everything was going swimmingly. Curtis kept halved 3X5 cards and a pen in his shirt pocket. When you alerted him to a problem, he would pull out a card and write down the problem right in front of you. I have no idea what he did with those cards, but the drama was enough to elevate him in the hearts and minds of his team.

On the other end of the scales was Rick. Late one January, he paid to fly the entire sales force to NY. As luck would have it, there was a terrible snow storm the night we all had to fly in to the event and between flight delays and cancellations, there was poor attendance. My delayed flight brought me to my hotel at 4 am. Rick arrived later and explained why with a long story about his wife and kids. He ended by saying. "See, us exec's have the same problems and issues as you all have. We are not so different than you."

Sure, I thought, we are exactly alike minus an extra zero in our paycheck. His appeal fell flat with me. He wanted the fame and money and none of the responsibility. He was short lived in his position and I have no idea what he is doing now.

I am not sure that either Curtis or Rick was more likely to do something about a great idea given to them. At TotalCom, the best anyone could hope for was to be heard. Change is something that comes of necessity or from outside influences. Innovation from within is not comprehended. Was it good enough for me just to be heard with my social selling ideas? I started to lose the confidence I had begun with eighteen months before. I started to wonder. Should I just give up? But I had walked a long way out onto this thin ice. Where was I to go from here? I could continue to use my secret weapon and sell even more. My vice president, Nicole, didn't even seem overly happy with the turnaround at Bluestar. Like Loni she saw sales as cyclical, and she saw the most potential personal risk when customers were buying more services not less. What if the sale team mis-sold the solution? What if the implementation went bad? Besides, she wanted to control the cadence and way things were sold, even if it meant less success. At TotalCom, failure together was better than success alone. Nicole became critical of our sales because we did not include the technology group at Bluestar in the decision. She talked about how dangerous that could be. After a decade of sales training costing the company millions, telling us to start selling to business people and not technology teams, Nicole found the water glass half-empty. But her goals were not to sell. She wanted sales success and good years, but creating new ways to propel the business forward was not her idea of success. She wanted to stay off the radar for any problems that might crop up due to a difficult implementation. She especially feared problems that she could not control but would require her involvement. Her involvement meant risk of failure or misstep. She could not control big, intense, emotional situations that included her management. In her mind, any emotional situation was an opportunity for failure. If she could keep the waters smooth, she would clinch her 30 year paycheck. She might even have an opportunity to move up if she kept all quiet in the southeast. In these ways, she was identical to Loni in Minneapolis. She met our first big sale to Bluestar with skepticism. How could we have made that happen so quickly? She hauled me into her office, closed the door and interrogated me, questioning me on what rules I broke to get the client to buy. She certainly was not singing my praises up the management line either.

But our senior execs were aware of the success and the turnaround at Bluestar. They wanted a write-up they could share with all of sales. I put the release together high-lighting the social media selling aspects. I sent it up the command chain. A few weeks later the release was blasted to the entire global sales team in our weekly newsletter. The release mentioned nothing about social media selling. Instead it concentrated on how our senior executives had helped to get the sale closed. The write up read like a 'Best Picture' speech at the Oscars. "I would like to thank..." It was safe. It lacked any imagination and it would not grab anyone's attention.

Chapter 13

How it all Ended

I had outperformed my greatest expectations, and TotalCom had found a way to bury my voice, bury my work and bury my success. But, really, was it TotalCom or my lingering sense of entitlement that made me feel disappointed? TotalCom owed me nothing and I owed it nothing back. Hadn't that been my realization when I moved to Atlanta and took my own approach? Really, was I doing this for TotalCom or for me? That answer was easy. I was doing this for me. So why did I expect TotalCom to notice at all?

One afternoon, as I pondered all this, I read an inspirational post on LinkedIn. It said, 'First aim high, and then aim higher.' Possibly, I needed to get above the fray with my idea to affect change in the organization. Have I mentioned that there is nothing more dangerous at a company like TotalCom than to go above you manager's head with a fresh idea?

A few months before, I had an idea to get a video produced to use with my social media efforts marketing to Bluestar. I knew that Nicole had no budget to do this and would see only obstacles if I asked. My mid-level management was scared to death of Nicole and wouldn't help. Nicole's boss, Andre, sat in NY and I had met him at a sales conference the previous fall. He listened to my ideas around social media at the conference. While he was not overly enthusiastic, he definitely did not seem like the kind of person who wanted to block the flow of good ideas. With this in mind, I emailed him my proposal for making a video. I asked for a half hour to discuss it and specifically asked how I could get on his calendar...yeah, right. I got a call later that day from Jessica who explained to me in a rote fashion how disappointed Nicole was that I had gone over her head. She was glad to hear my idea, but I should never take anything to Andre without first telling everyone in the management chain of command first. Andre did not even deign to respond to my inquiry.

"Aim high and then aim higher", I think I see the wisdom in that. Is there anyone at TotalCom who is above the gravitational forces of the 30 year paycheck? Is there anyone not in the play-it-safe-at-all-times club? I decided to find out. The head of retail sales was a relic. He had been carrying a sales bag since the days when sales people actually carried bags. He was also Andre's boss. I thought about him and quickly realized he would be a bad target to talk to about modernizing anything, let alone his precious sales force. The head of retail sales reported up to the CEO Nigel. Nigel had a very approachable manner. Nigel was a 'thinking' and refined version of Curtis (the guy with the half sheets of 3X5 cards in his shirt pocket). By chance, I had asked a slew of Total-Com executives to connect with me on the LinkedIn social media site. This was an early experiment I did right after I was 'reassigned' by Loni. Nigel was one of the few who accepted my invitation to connect. I think Nigel took the approach to link with anyone at TotalCom at that time. Who knows what his thinking was, but there I was in direct contact with our CEO on social media. Needless to say there were few who attempted to link with the top management. What good could possibly come out of it?

I reasoned I had nothing to lose. Wasn't this why I came to Atlanta to begin with? I intended to shake things up to see what would happen. I couldn't be held down or scared by the TotalCom mystique anymore. Also, it was clear that working under Nicole was not a recipe for me to get promoted. My smack down from Loni and my time spent in the corporate penalty box had certainly been viewed as not long enough. I hardly acted contrite or safe. Who was I kidding anyway? I had exactly zero upper level sponsors. My ideas and inability to shut up made me a liability. Despite the revenue I had brought in, my sales successes meant that I needed to be tolerated, but kept at arm's length. I certainly wasn't making friends in Atlanta. I didn't come here to make friends and it was about to get worse.

As I had already demonstrated with my email to Andre, one sure way to get smacked down was by launching an email to the top brass. Executive Assistants at Nigel's level made sure that guys like him never even saw a message from a guy like me. My experience with Andre was not some novel approach he had invented. It was a learned response carved out of Totalcom's corporate culture. Andre's response was textbook for keeping his position and moving closer to collecting his 30 year paycheck.

But what would happen if I messaged an executive via LinkedIn? It was a personal network message, not corporate email. Just like a letter sent to your home. It would be hard for an executive to take a birthday card they got in their mailbox and send it to the middle management and say, "why is this guy pestering me?" By the same token, it is hard to chide someone who sends a note via LinkedIn. The note never becomes a proper email, so what is there to object to? My motto had always been that "I have a network for a reason" and I planned to use the people I knew to help my career.

LinkedIn was the perfect weapon. The old school culture that resisted my social selling ideas had not counted on how social media might allow an infiltration into the top ranks.

I sent the CEO a simple note asking if he would like to see my report on how we won the Bluestar contracts. It was irresistible. Just like Bluestar's business unit leaders, Nigel was intrigued. He asked for my report that included all the social media aspects of the sale, and I sent it. He forwarded it to the Chief Marketing Officer (CMO) with a stern note, "we need to do more of this.." I was placed in copy on that note. I saw my opportunity and reached out to the CMO to discuss my idea. I had never been so prepared for a discussion. The CMO scheduled fifteen minutes for us to talk and I was finished giving him my story in seven minutes flat. I had even included my pitch to create and run a new division in social sales. He kept me on the phone for the full half hour, giving me his ideas. He asked me what I honestly thought. He had a lot of old school ideas on vertical markets. I told him I did not think they would work without infusing a more genuine and sales-focused approach like the one I used at Bluestar.

I had a next step ready, just in case the CMO wanted to sweep me under the rug. A very old trick to get an underling back in line and to give up on his quest, is to agree to meet with him, listen intently and then leave before a next step could be determined. This is the equivalent of killing a bill in committee. Minimally, it stalled any idea from reaching critical mass.

I told the CMO I wanted to head up a new team that would experiment and try social approaches with our customers. I even had accounts and account managers briefed and ready to give it a try. I then directly asked if he wanted to proceed to the next step which was a formal presentation. He chuckled at first. I persisted. He got quiet and then relented. "Ok, let's do that", he said. I got off the phone...fast. Victory! Or so it seemed. I spent the next few weeks putting together a single paged plan that fit onto an 11X17 sheet showing all the aspects of my program including individual tactics, deliverables and the central reason we were doing this--to replicate the $50 million sale at Bluestar. I sent the CMO the document via overnight mail and emailed him to find some more time to discuss. I got no response, but that was normal. At least I had come to believe that not responding to a request to meet was normal.

Not responding to a phone call or email is an option for anyone above your pay grade. I have come to understand that this is not an act of rudeness, but rather an act of fear. Nothing good can come of answering difficult questions in writing. Since evading those questions with any response becomes part of the public record, it is easier not to respond at all. For example, I included a story about Loni in a blog post I wrote my first year in Atlanta. I sent her a note with the web link to the post, asking what she thought. Her response read like a postcard from the beach. "Hi, how are you? Hope you are well"

Ha, ha, ha.

But really, it is quite sad. It is the emotional response of someone who is ultimately afraid to make a decision that may interfere with her own career prospects. The trouble is that when an entire organization plays by that rule, new thinking is virtually disallowed. I continued to ping the CMO with no response.

I thought through my options and possible outcomes.

The first option-- the CMO responded and was positive about my idea. He offered me a job in marketing and I live happily ever after. That sounded good. I knew that would frost the entire management structure in sales worse than any other outcome. It would prove that going above and around people led to success. Not a good habit to promote.

The second option-- the CMO did not respond. I would remain safe with management and everything remained the same. My reward would be to go on with the Bluestar account and look for my next big sale.

But something else was at stake this time. I had spent the past eighteen months doing it my way. I had forsaken the TotalCom culture in order to try something new. I had had an incredible success. Friends on my social channels were falling over themselves to get my story, have me cross-post on their blog and interview me. I was even asked to compete in a Social Selling contest which chose my story as a finalist. I was a celebrity with my story outside my company. My company, however, chose to kill all stories that did not include the current culture. No wonder change from within is always so difficult.

I asked myself if I was ready to pack it all in. Was I ready to forget what had happened and sit back down in my chair and eat my peas? And then what? One more year toward my 30 year paycheck. But nothing was adding up for me. I imagined the day I retired. Would I look back on this moment as a decision point? How would I view myself if I played it safe one more time?

But what alternatives did I have? I had thought about quitting many times, but finding a job was tough and the company knew it. They also knew that people don't save so they cannot quit. Corporate employees are the equivalent of modern day sharecroppers. Our move to Atlanta had wiped out our savings in the bank, but the reserves in my heart had grown tenfold.

Besides, by remaining true to myself, I had discovered something new. I had cracked a code on selling by using social media. I didn't exactly know it at the time, but I had created a new product, a new methodology. I had created something I could sell.

It was time to burn the last bridge. I walked into Jessica's office with a stack of printed emails. These were the email exchanges I was having with our CEO and CMO. I dropped them on her desk. She looked surprised. Just for good measure I included an exchange I had had with the Mayor of Atlanta...a contact I had made via a blog post I had done a month or so before. I self-anointed myself czar of social media and showed her my report on the Bluestar sales that tied the wins back to my social media methods. I could see her mind was racing. "Who else knows about this?" Who else in our sales division, was what she meant. She was assessing her own risk in this situation. Predictable.

"No one," I replied and invited her to share it with whomever she wanted. I knew this meant minimally a certain banishment to an outer recess of the organization until I could learn to comply with the rules of the road. It felt like I had lit a cigarette, put on a blindfold and stumbled out in front of a line of armed soldiers. I told Jessica I was sure the CMO was going to hire me into a job in his marketing team and I wanted to let her know what was happening. She was pleasant and upbeat a usual, but the next conversation I had with her boss, Allen, was not so pleasant.

His tack to get me back in line was to find fault with my current work. It was the biggest case of amnesia I had ever seen. He asked me how much time I was spending pushing my social media ideas and demanded I get back to work on Bluestar in earnest. I told him I wanted to replicate the Bluestar success. As is often the case when conversations get sticky at TotalCom, Allen conceded that he had no problem with what I was doing, but said that his boss did. Once upon a time I had heard Loni say back in Minnesota "I got a boss, you got a boss, all God's children have a boss" updating a line from an old song 'I Got Shoes'. What she meant was that everyone, except the CEO and the last hire, is really a middle manager at TotalCom and has to be concerned with and do the bidding of a superior. This is exactly the card Allen played. But it made no difference to me. He pleaded that if I had good ideas they needed to go to his boss, Nicole, and then up the chain. I retorted that if I had iron clad plans for a cold fusion reactor that would eliminate mankind's energy needs, Nicole would find a way to bury it. He smiled. "Why are you working here? We have a culture and rules here. You should go and become the chief innovation officer someplace."

How it all Ended

I appreciated the permission, but I had already mentally done so. My 30 year paycheck was over. The sense of freedom and peace I felt was overwhelming. Leaving this dysfunctional family for good now seemed to be the right move.

I was offered a job in our sales marketing group a day later. Getting away from Bluestar seemed logical for everyone. At first, I did not accept the offer. Allen had another conversation with me and I realized it made sense to take the job while I finalized my plans to leave for good. My new vice president wanted to talk to me before offering me the job.

She stammered over the phone line. "Andre wanted me to talk to you about something. He was very upset by the phone calls and emails or LinkedIn messages you have been sending. Andre is a great guy, and an excellent leader, but you know the culture around here. We need to stick together. I mean, what would happen if everybody went to the CEO with their good ideas..." I gave that one a good hard think. I envisioned a very different TotalCom. It was a TotalCom beyond the safety of a paycheck and a job in perpetuity. Frankly, I couldn't believe she was saying this. "...Andre wanted me to tell you that there would be no more sending of emails--including LinkedIn messages..." (It was interesting to hear that TotalCom's culture now included limitations on social media too.) "...and, if you do not listen, Andre said he was going to get you." That sounded ominous. Get me. Get me what?

The amazing thing about TotalCom was that no matter what kind of tough words people use, everyone is part of the same machine. Even a guy at Andre's level couldn't just fire someone who wasn't crossing over human resources guidelines. The culture of fear being breached was not a dismissible offense. It just meant that you would never prosper and everyone would treat you poorly until you finally had to quit or the next layoff rolled around and it was expedient to put you on the 'unsafe' list. In other words, you are rejected like a sliver, slowly, painfully and purposefully. I laughed at the notion of Andre firing me for bringing new ideas to the CEO. I obediently agreed to be good boy.

A few days later Nicole wanted to speak with me. Her message was similar. Andre had asked her to talk with me before I took the new job. Nicole used the analogy of 'swimming in the lanes.' I was never much good at that, having learned to swim in a deep lake in upstate New York. Nicole's line went like this: "I know you have good ideas, but we're a big company..." What was this supposed to mean? Nicole was indicating that creativity was not needed here or wanted? Her modus operandi belied this. She always looked for the problem instead of dreaming of the solution. Her safety conscious mind barked out commands to put on a belt with your suspenders in any situation instead of daring to do the impossible, to dream big, to win decisively.

But for Nicole as well as Loni or anyone else real or imagined who has graced the pages of this book, freedom from the 30 year paycheck has always been within reach. I didn't need to quit to find it. What I did learn after twenty years of being afraid was, there was no reason to be afraid to begin with. My job, my chance of promotion, the security of my group or division did not rely on me being afraid and taking the most secure path at all times. My success actually relied on the opposite. The culture of fear is not the culture that started TotalCom many years ago, but it is certainly the culture that could destroy it, along with many other businesses just like it.

I was just having coffee with a woman who worked for a very well respected retail brand. She told me that the corporate culture when she began with her employer was so wonderful that no one wanted to ever leave. People worked there for 30 or 40 years. But something happened on the way into the Information Age. Corporations forgot the social contract they had written with their employees. They continued to talk about it as existing, but they started treating employees as if they were widgets in a factory. This quickly killed the culture of innovation and replaced it with one of fear and repression. Coloring outside the lines couldn't make anyone valuable in a culture of parts and pieces. Not only did it stifle anyone from being creative, it created an environment that shunned and removed anyone who exhibited these traits. Self-selection created a culture of a huddled mass hoping to weather any storm and continue to collect a paycheck. Like rearranging the deck chairs on the Titanic, these organizations move pieces around, struggling to survive. As long as nothing new is introduced, everyone can feel safe and sound.

But market forces are bigger than any corporation's pocketbook. Change is inevitable. Perhaps one employee can collect a few more years of paychecks than another by angling properly, but any sense of security is a false one. Innovation is a necessary part of long term success. Understandably, younger workers are choosing not to work at large companies. Since the last recession many large companies have been loath to hire anyone, so potentially the feeling is mutual. But if younger people do not come to work for these behemoths, who will be working there in twenty years? This problem should take care of itself and market forces will prevail, but my point is that anyone playing the game of fear and safety in a company like TotalCom has probably more to worry about (and less chance of hitting that higher income bracket) than a starving entrepreneur working out of a warehouse. Just look at how the top management of companies like TotalCom covet those innovators.

The Coca-cola Company has recently set up internal start-up labs that include teams of employees who work away from the rest of the corporate culture in start-up company space with start-up company rules and culture. The importance of corporate labs where new prod-ucts are conceived under a different culture has recently skyrocketed. 'Innovation' is a word clouded in jealousy and desire in boardrooms from coast to coast. "Where do we find it and how much will it cost?" business leaders ask as if innovation is a resource that can be mined or produced with a solid business plan.

It took me twenty years to see the illusion. It took me many heartaches to bring me to my senses about what was going on. The most important person I can ever be is me. I am enough. In fact, I am more than enough. My ideas set me apart from everyone else, just as yours set you apart from the rest of us too. By giving up that one unique quality for the promise of a 30 year paycheck, our very core is at stake. Don't do it. They can keep the 30 year paycheck. You and I are more important than that. On the first of October that year I resigned. Nicole was surprised. She asked me, "Are you sure?" I was sure.

Chapter 14

Conclusion

The fundamental question remains, what can individuals and companies do to create an improved workplace for everyone? How can employees avoid being trapped in a 30 year paycheck quagmire? How can employers stop creating life-squelching environments and departments that create 30 year paycheck employees to begin with?

First, what can we do as employees? Sometime during the 1950's, the contract with corporate workers changed. The post-industrial revolution created a world where employees valued their company over their co-workers. They began to feel protected by their company. The company wrote them a paycheck each week and gave them a yearly bonus. As strange as it may sound, we started to forget that a business or corporation is really a bunch of people who come to work each day for a common cause and a shared set of objectives. In our amnesia, several things resulted. First, we started to view our co-workers as the enemy, the people we needed to beat out for a promotion, the boss who kept our good ideas at bay, the direct report who showed up late and did not make good on a commitment. The organization quickly was divided into fiefdoms where personal curry outweighed value to the corporation.

THE 30 YEAR PAYCHECK

I went to a weekly lunch held at a local tech start-up company incubator. These office buildings are springing up everywhere with support from local governments and business hell-bent on making their city the next Silicon Valley. At this lunch, I looked at all the twenty-somethings laughing and eating pizza. They are making minimum wage or sometimes less, but they toil late hours and seem to have honest interest in the welfare of each other. Why wasn't it like this in my office? One big difference is that each of these kids owns shares in the company. If they are ever bought out, those shares will potentially be worth big money. But the competition is fierce and there is only so much acquisition money in corporate America. Winning this game is a team sport and you can see that on their faces at the lunch table. They want to win, together.

The second thing we forgot in our amnesia is that the corporation was created to make money and grow. I used to write Shakespearean expense reports that explained in minute detail how all my travels and lunches would ultimately 'bring in new revenue to TotalCom, and drive shareholder value.' Everyone got a good laugh out of them, but I had a serious mission in mind. I felt that too many people misused company expenses to promote their own career and pad their own frequent flyer and hotel rewards accounts. Entitlement, for the long hours or for being overlooked for a promotion or for the measly bonus that year based on poor results. "Those results weren't my fault, I certainly did my part!", they probably rationalized. I wanted to affirm with my expense reports that I was working for the benefit of our common goals—corporate profits. I also wanted to say that we may not meet our objectives, but I

Conclusion

was doing my part to try. I stood like an island with my expense reports. Eventually, I stopped.

In both cases of amnesia, the remedy is really quite simple. Corporate employees need to wake up. As employees we must remind ourselves what we are doing for the firm and why. I believe many corporate workers stay in a job title far too long. This distorts reality as the purpose of their job in making the corporation function is forgotten. The individual becomes the position. The personality is the function. It is one of the main reasons we start to feel entitled, too.

But if we stay focused on what we are doing, and whether that job has relevance to the organization, there is a twofold advantage. We keep a sense of purpose in what we do each day. Not that every task we do could win us the Nobel Peace Prize, but that overall we are making a difference each day for our co-workers and for ourselves. How many corporate workers today believe that their presence in the office actually helps the others in the department, let alone helps the company make payroll each week? Imagine if they did? Would a vice president ever chide a first line manager for taking good ideas that could help the company to the chief executive officer? Or might he take the ideas up the ladder himself, giving credit where credit is due.

Also, when we adopt this attitude of greater purpose in the organization, we better know when it is time to change jobs. I think there is far too little self-directed change happening inside corporations. People stay put, make their alliances and begin fighting a battle inside the corporate walls. Soon, the foot soldiers forget their self-worth beyond girding for the next internal attack. They figure they cannot be worthy of anything beyond the current framework and if they are they will certainly be tapped on the shoulder and told when it is time for a promotion. They travel in packs with those whom they have forged alliances. While this may be a safe route, it is not life-affirming for the employee. The employee loses a sense of control. I believe we all need to regain that control. This means we need to stay empowered. There is much of corporate structure that needs to change, but try to imagine a world with more decisive employees. First, they would perform their functions in a way that uses all the intelligence and experience they possess. Empowered to make decisions, the decisions made would put the corporation's best interest at heart. Making the safe personal decision naturally ranks lower to the employee who doesn't expect to be in the same job for the next ten years or who is not worried about how they rank in advance of the next layoff. Learning, making mistakes and creating a better company rewards everyone in the end.

Empowered employees also know when it is time to move on. I was blocked from making changes when I lost the drive to be a sales manager. Middle management felt it couldn't reward me with a new position both because it would be difficult to replace me, and they felt I wasn't doing an exceptional job. Apart from overt slacking, anyone not doing a good job in a present position should be given the latitude to find a better fit. A fit that will match their passions and abilities. Sometimes that fit will not necessarily exist. It is the job of the corporate structure to be flexible or allow the employee to gracefully leave. Leaving a company has a stigma for many 30 year paycheckers. They believe others will assume the worst about them. Still others will believe that they don't know how to survive. Or that they are stupid for not being able to move up in the company. Or that they have no worth.

Another force that keeps employees from leaving even when it makes sense is the fear they will not be able to find another job. Skills matter. We all have them, but if we do not exercise them it can appear as if we don't. The key is to continue to exercise our skills, forget the politics and push ourselves to fulfill the core mission of our company and our personal destiny. We are here for just a short while. There is no reason to waste time waiting. The longer we wait the harder it is to awaken from the haze of a 30 year paycheck. We all need to work as if the money is not the goal, and the money will sort itself out. What is the price of happiness, anyway?

As for the organizational structure and operations of corporations, there are many things that can be done to give employees the needed empowerment and freedom to innovate. In so doing a culture of 30 year paycheck workers can be avoided.

First, allow employees to do their passion. I am not saying that corporations should pander to the employee's whims, but rather that they create an environment that values the unique ways each person approaches any given task. I roam the halls of large corporations these days and see large banners with corporate 'rules of the road' hanging everywhere. It is amazing how similar they are to one another, especially those of arch rivals. 'Act with integrity', 'be direct with people', 'do what you say you are going to do', I think they all came out of some McKinsey management consulting handbook on how to fix dysfunctional organizations. What would happen if the first corporate guideline was, 'We are all unique, use our diversity, skills and ideas to build a better company'? Would a company with this flying on a thirty foot banner in the cafeteria ever breed vice presidents who choose to play it safe over making a difference? This one value could propel the innovators up the management chain and build a renaissance business that would never run out of ideas.

Randall Stephenson, Chairman of AT&T, publically states that he is always looking for the next billion dollar business. Without fostering an environment where new and different ideas are encouraged, I wonder where he hopes to find the inspiration. The employee payroll is the single biggest expense for most companies. By spending millions with consulting firms to buy innovation, the investment in salaries is wasted. What if employees were allowed to take on 'special assignments' in other departments through a program sponsored by Human Resources to build diversity? What if a 'study abroad' type program was instituted that gave employees a chance to work overseas in international operations? What if human resources started to actively place individuals in new roles at all levels in the company and pushed back on a good-old-boy network of hiring based on gut instincts and friendships? Perhaps human resources could spend less time convincing the rank and file why they want to stay. Breaking these bonds in middle management by rotating new managers in and out of roles at the vice president and senior vice president level is extremely important to creating empowered employees. If no one feels trapped in a 30 year paycheck, no one will have a motive to repress others. I watched as countless vice presidents held onto roles for ten, twenty or more years. Those organizations most resembled the fiefdoms of favor and least embodied a spirit of human empowerment. The counter argument is that these long term managers are operationally sound and will do the best job in these roles. But this argument assumes a fundamental difference in how employees are regarded. Are we being asked by the company to perform a task or are we being called upon to innovate and continually change the business? In the Information Age, it seems extremely out dated to value experience over empowerment and innovation. The top executives already know this and that is why there is a huge push for new ideas in the first place.

Businesses also need to rethink what type of relationship they have with their employees. Since the post-industrial era, corporations have tried to convince employees that they are part of a family. The only problem is, it is not a very safe or loving family. Sure, employees get paid days off and health insurance benefits, but when it behooves the corporation, the business regularly jettisons workers based on the 'needs of the business climate.' Furthermore, there are absolutely no guarantees that if workers do good work and stay with the firm that the company will promote them or care for them when times are hard. Corporations would be much better off to go back to an old school relationship that looks like a 'day's wages for a day's work'. Here's why. First, the inconsistency that is created when employees are told they are family and then get treated like hourly workers creates mistrust and a penchant to always do what is safe. It stifles the company. The more it stifles, the more layoffs occur. And the layoffs create more worker mistrust in a vicious cycle. Second, families are complicated units. Yes, emotional bonds are extremely strong and can drive a small group to do much more than the sum of its parts. But the flip side is that families also act irrationally. Feuds develop, and accommodations are made for individuals who perform poorly or abuse others. There is no room for this in a corporation. Why can't we be honest with each other? A corporation hires a human being to help perform the mission of the company. The role of the individual is to provide her entire mind to creating more value and profit for the business. In return, the worker is paid money. Loyalty is created by offering a worker an environment in which she can learn and grow. It is just the opposite of the 30 year paycheck. Loyalty for a 30 year paycheck worker is created by fear and by encouraging an employee to resort to tricks in order to keep her around. It may sound like more work to create an environment of empowerment, but the benefits are huge. Workers who are loyal because the company looks for ways to validate their uniqueness and need to grow, are far more valuable than workers who are loyal because they are afraid to take risks, be creative and challenge the status quo. Again, the trade-off is that corporations must also be willing to grow. It means that companies must face their own mortality along with the mortality of people who work there.

The cycle of birth, growth and eventual death is everywhere. So why is it that we assume companies should have the privilege of living forever with the same ideals, goals and products? In the human body, a cell that refuses to die is often deemed cancerous. It is our own desire to create safety where none exists that we suppress change. By being honest about the relationship between worker and corporation, we are

Conclusion

affirming that nothing lasts forever and we are offering anyone with the desire, the empowerment to help create a new dawn.

Corporations looking to avoid the pitfalls of the 30 year paycheck must also continuously ask for feedback. As worker dissatisfaction started to mount in the 1980's, a new industry around collecting feedback from employees was born. Businesses were told to involve employees in how the corporation could improve and they could win back loyalty and job appreciation. I remember a co-worker who filled out his annual feedback form with the tirade, "no one looks at these stupid things anyway" My co-worker got a personal email from the vice president assuring him that he did read them! We all got a big chuckle out of this, but I got to thinking about it. It was good to hear that our vice president read the responses, but I think the complaint was that nothing was ever fundamentally changed based on the feedback. Again, a culture where changing the organization and bringing in new voices regularly will upset middle management. This paradigm needs to be eliminated. Feedback that will be a blueprint to completely recreate the organization should be actively sought. Additionally, the team creating the blueprint needs to ask themselves if they are right for the new job titles and functions being created. Everyone needs to know that jobs are temporary and that they need to be constantly thinking about what they will do next. Everyone in the corporation needs to be accountable for the ideas and feedback to make sure the job they want to grow into will be there for them. Each department needs to be constantly asking itself, "In what ways are we bringing the firm into a viable and better future?" Thousands of pages have been written about the importance of corporate culture. Simply put, every corporate culture needs to be built around finding new ideas and bringing them to fruition quickly. Planning for new business integration needs to take the back seat to creating the innovation in the first place.

If you are a Chief Executive Officer, take more risks. Shareholders may not like it, but how does death by one thousand one-point stock losses beat a single large dip? By playing it safe, the incremental losses are almost certain and big gains will never come. Compare Apple or Google to any Dow Jones company. Change needs to start at the top. I have recently worked with a company that was almost left for dead after a failed take-over attempt and has come back from the ashes. It is now changing all the rules in the market. The business is thriving. More importantly for the future, the employees feel empowered. They feel that the change they are creating in the market is their battle too. They are applying all their intelligence to make it happen. The empowerment I have witnessed at this company is marvelous. Anyone would want to be part of it. And it can be sustained as long as the culture permits employee empowerment.

With the help of some of these tactics, we can rid the world of 30 year paycheck employees. That is not to say that employees will never work for one employer for 30 years. It just means that employees will remain empowered and growing their entire career. Simply giving an employee a gold watch in return for minimal effort and the safest of actions for three decades doesn't honor anyone. I know it is not a secret that thousands of beaten souls inhabit the office buildings of every downtown in America. There is a way to free them, to make them better.

Conclusion

And this leads to better businesses too. But to do so means companies can no longer guard human capital and lock it away in a cell. The best companies in the next 30 years will benefit from their work force by letting it move and grow freely and by allowing it to produce lasting and continuous change.

Epilogue

I traded my cube for this nice window seat in the lower level of my mid-century Atlanta home. This is my new office. The view out of the window isn't much. It is mostly taken up by the trunk of an enormous pin oak tree. But each day a squirrel climbs down from above and chews his acorns and looks in at me. I often wonder what he is thinking. I must seem to him to be a curious exhibit behind a pane of glass. Behind me is a couch that is the demilitarized zone between my office space and the kids play area. At present, plastic crocodiles are munching on neon orange plastic lobsters at the base of a large tower of wooden blocks.

Today I consult with large and small companies alike on many of the principles I have shared in this book. I find myself traveling a lot more than I ever have, but the nice trade-off is that when I am home, I am truly home. My business, Thought Horizon, is dedicated to changing the 30 year paycheck syndrome. My work is now my passion and vice versa. I feel extremely fortunate to have found the path to this place. Each day as I help others along the way, I am reminded of that.

Acknowledgments

I wish to thank the following individuals for their help in making this book possible: Julie Gibson Biehn, Chris Biehn, Matthew Stecker, John Haldi, Nan Salberg and Senour Reed. Book design and cover illustration was done by Linda Olliver. Mike Olliver is responsible for the photograph on the back cover.

29842012R00156

Made in the USA
Charleston, SC
25 May 2014